BEST OF
SMALL GROUPS
Volume I

BEST OF
SMALL GROUPS

Volume 1

12 Small Group Bible Studies

Randy Alcorn

Francis Chan

Mark Driscoll

Kyle Idleman

Chip Ingram

Max Lucado & Randy Frazee

Erwin McManus

Miles McPherson

Don Piper

John Piper

Kerry Shook

Gary Smalley

HENDRICKSON PUBLISHERS

lifetogether
EVERYTHING SMALL GROUPS

The Best of Small Groups Volume I

© 2012 by Hendrickson Publishers Marketing, LLC
P.O. Box 3473
Peabody, Massachusetts 01961-3473

ISBN 978-1-59856-846-2

All rights reserved. No part of this book may be reproduced or transmitted in any form or by any means, electronic or mechanical, including photocopying, recording, or by any information storage and retrieval system, without permission in writing from the publisher.

Please see the pages at the end of this workbook for additional permission statements.

Printed in the United States of America

First Printing — September 2012

Contents

Introduction ... 7
Overview ... 8

Disk One

SESSION ONE — "Making Room for Life," from *Making Room for Neighbors*, Max Lucado and Randy Frazee ... 9

SESSION TWO — "I've Got Jesus. Why Do I Need the Spirit?" from *Forgotten God*, Francis Chan ... 16

SESSION THREE — "Is Jesus the Only God?" from *Vintage Jesus*, Mark Driscoll ... 25

SESSION FOUR — "Fan or Follower?" from *Not a Fan*, Kyle Idleman ... 31

SESSION FIVE — "Does God Care?" from *Life's Toughest Questions*, Erwin McManus ... 38

SESSION SIX — "The Fight for Joy Is Essential (Part 1)," from *When I Don't Desire God*, John Piper ... 47

Disk Two

SESSION SEVEN — "Do You Have a Plan?" from *Guarding Your Child's Heart*, Gary Smalley ... 50

SESSION EIGHT — "The Plan," from *DO Something!* Miles McPherson ... 60

SESSION NINE — "What We Know about Heaven," from *Heaven*, Randy Alcorn ... 73

SESSION TEN — "Living the Dash," from *One Month to Live*, Kerry and Chris Shook ... 83

SESSION ELEVEN — "God's Dream for Your Life," from *Living on the Edge*, Chip Ingram ... 91

SESSION TWELVE — "Heaven in the Next Instant?" from *90 Minutes in Heaven*, Don Piper ... 96

BONUS SESSION — "Becoming a Celebrating Community," from *Building Biblical Community*, Steve Gladen and Bill Donahue ... 103

APPENDIX

Small Group FAQs	110
Small Group Covenant	111
Small Group Calendar	113
Small Group Roster	114
Circles of Life	115
Prayer and Praise Report	116

Introduction

Welcome to *The Best of Small Groups*!

As a small group member and curriculum developer, I have been amazed at the recent explosion of interest in small groups, the ever-expanding development of resources, and the commitment on the part of many churches to the special role that small groups have in the lives of Jesus' followers. The need for teaching and fellowship is not entirely met in large group gatherings or by individual spiritual pursuits. Jesus spent time by Himself and He spoke to large gatherings of followers, but He invested the greatest amount of time with the small group He called His disciples. That pattern remains essential to today's Christians.

If you are a small group leader, the variety, approach, and style of available small group curricula can seem mind-boggling. Most major Christian authors are involved to one degree or another in the creation of video-based materials that help small groups engage with their message. Because there are so many great resources available, small groups leaders are likely to be overwhelmed at the choices to be made. And since most of us don't spend all our time evaluating video study materials, a great deal of what is available simply never shows up on our radar.

Enter *The Best of Small Groups*. Its new approach seeks to expose leaders and small groups to a wider variety of content than they may discover using the hit-or-miss approach. Each of the authors and studies featured in this first volume has been recognized as a wonderful resource on the Christian life. Although you may not be familiar with all the names represented, I encourage you to sample those teachers. You may well discover a crucial theme or an interesting approach that would be helpful for your small group. One or more of these studies may already be familiar to you, but even if your group has gone through that particular study, turnover and the need for review may lead you to take your group through sample sessions they have already experienced.

In all cases, I trust you will find each of these sessions an invitation to further exploration in the challenging world of Bible lessons and small group interaction. Take your group boldly where they have not gone before, knowing God will be there to meet you!

Brett Eastman

Overview

The twelve studies featured in this volume include some of the biggest names and best-selling studies in Christianity today, as well as a few rising stars. Each of the twelve studies is the first session in its series. To give you the best taste of each series, we have kept the sessions as close to the originals as possible.

At the end of every session we have added a section titled "More Information about This Study." It includes bibliographic and availability notes for the larger study from which each sample session is taken, as well as information about companion books and resources that accompany the full study.

The videos for the sessions in this study guide are a part of a two-DVD set. Sessions 1 through 6 are on DVD 1 and sessions 7 through 12, including the bonus session, are on DVD 2. Lifetogether has also included a training video for leaders, called a "Leader Lifter," with each of the sessions. They can be accessed from each session menu as well as from the "Leader Lifters" menus on both DVDs.

SESSION ONE
Making Room for Neighbors

Making Room for Life
by Max Lucado and Randy Frazee

Do you know your neighbors? Most people live such busy lives that they really have no room left to connect with the people next door. Whether you have good neighbors, bad neighbors, or anonymous neighbors, God placed you in your neighborhood for a reason.

The light of Christ shines through the life of every believer. Before you flip to the next lesson out of fear of some awkward evangelistic strategy, please understand that relationship is the start of God's work through you to the lives of your neighbors. Your presence in their lives is significant. This session will show you why.

INTRODUCTION

The Story Behind the Neighborhood

The group that meets in Randy's neighborhood is nearing sixty people. Although it took Randy and Rozanne over fourteen months developing relationships before their gatherings began, they knew from experience that true community can't be rushed. Randy has spent almost ten years using the neighborhood model to strengthen communities of all kinds. Whether your neighborhood is large or small, urban or rural, this method is proven to work.

Would you be willing to begin praying and taking practical steps to start fostering your own relationships with your neighbors? By hosting a barbecue or other neighborhood activities with the young and old alike, you will become better prepared to host your own neighborhood gatherings.

"As long as the earth endures, seedtime and harvest, cold and heat, summer and winter, day and night will never cease" (Genesis 8:22 NIV).

COMING TOGETHER

If this is your first time together as a group, there are some important things to discuss. It's always fun to take some time getting to know one another. Does everyone know everyone else's name? Here are a few ideas you can use to break the ice as you begin this series.

1 My Best Year
Here you can take your choice: tell us about the best year you ever had and what made it special, or tell us what your dream vacation would be if there were no limitations (e.g., children, work, schedules, outside commitments)?

_____
_____
_____
_____

2 How Did You Get Here?
Invite everyone to briefly share how they came to live in this neighborhood. Where did they move from and why did they decide on this little corner of the globe to establish a home?

_____
_____
_____
_____

3 My Immediate Neighborhood
On a large piece of paper or poster board, draw a simple map of your street with the five or six homes that are closest to yours. Label them with as many of the names of the people who live in each home as you can remember. Take time before the next session to fill in the blanks.

_____
_____
_____
_____
_____

LEARNING TOGETHER

Roll Tape: DVD Session One

Learning Together (notes)

The section below provides you some open space to write down your reactions, reflections, and resolutions based on the teaching and testimonies. As you listen, write down your thoughts and be prepared to discuss them later.

_____
_____
_____
_____
_____
_____
_____
_____
_____
_____
_____

Possible Components of a Neighborhood Gathering

- Mingling
- Circling for Prayer
- Sharing a Meal
- Bible Reading
- Praying Over Shared Concerns
- Journaling the Journey
- Planning for Service Opportunities

Action Step 1
Be intentional about how you approach neighbors

GROWING TOGETHER

Reflect on some of what you heard and saw during the video segments. Offer your own thoughts to the group, using some or all of the following questions:

1 What is one new thing you want to start doing and one thing you want to stop doing in order to be more intentional this next season?

_____
_____
_____

2 Take a moment to write down three to five items that you will share with someone else a week from now.

_____
_____
_____

3 What is one way you have been intentional with your seasons in past years?

_____
_____
_____

Deeper Bible Study

Your group may want to look at the biblical background of this session's emphasis on making room for a different schedule and realigned priorities this year. The following two passages allow us not only to think about Jesus in community, but also about the ways He taught His followers to view people around them.

Matthew 9:35–38 "Seeing the Neighborhood"

1. Jesus combined two different pictures into one when He looked at the crowds that came to be with Him. What was the idea, and what does it mean to see people that way?

_____
_____
_____
_____
_____

2. In what ways does your view of your immediate neighbors include the possibility that some of them are "found" and some of them are "lost"? What choices do these possibilities create for you?

3. How would praying for your neighbors by name and need begin to change the depth of your perception of them and your relationship with them?

See also Luke 19:41–44; Exodus 20:16–17

Luke 24:13–35 — "Hosting Jesus"

1. After walking and talking with Jesus on the road to Emmaus, what made the men invite Jesus to stay the evening? When you spend meaningful time with Jesus, do you tend to assume you're leaving Him behind when that's over or that you are taking Him with you as you move on?

2. What distinct actions of Jesus did God use to open the eyes of the men who were hosting Him in Emmaus? How do you recognize the signs that Jesus is working in your life or in someone else's life?

3. In what ways would you like to see your relationship with Jesus significantly change for the better this next year? What will those changes require from you?

See also Deuteronomy 6:4–9, 20–25

SHARING TOGETHER

Suggestions for practical application based on the conversation of the session:

My Dreams

Take a moment to think about and then record below what you consider to be your three most significant dreams for reaching out to your neighborhood.

1 _____

2 _____

3 _____

Discuss what should go on the Neighborhood Calendar. Discuss ways you can "safeguard" certain dates, times, and occasions for the kinds of priorities Randy and Max are talking about.

Talk through the elements that Randy mentioned were part of the neighborhood gathering: mingling, circling for prayer, sharing a meal, Bible reading, praying over shared concerns, journaling the journey, and planning for service opportunities. Choose one or two of these to incorporate in this group as you go forward.

HINT FOR NEXT TIME

If the whole idea of making a significant lifestyle change intrigues you, you might want to read Randy Frazee's book, *Making Room for Life*.

MORE INFORMATION ABOUT THIS STUDY

This sample is the first session from the series *Making Room for Neighbors*, a five-session DVD study by Max Lucado and Randy Frazee. The study guides and DVDs are published by Hendrickson Publishers and available online through Christian Book Distributors or at your local Christian bookstore.

Authors

Max Lucado is the only author to have won three Christian Book of the Year awards—in 1999 for *Just Like Jesus*, in 1997 for *In the Grip of Grace*, and in 1995 for *When God Whispers Your Name*. In 2005, *Reader's Digest* dubbed him "America's Best Preacher," and in 2004, *Christianity Today* called him "America's Pastor." The product line for *3:16—The Numbers of Hope* sold more than four million units worldwide, including one million units of the cornerstone trade book of the same title (released in September 2007), making it the fastest-selling product in Lucado's career. His latest book, *Outlive Your Life: You Were Made to Make a Difference* (September 2010), hit both the *Publishers Weekly* and *New York Times* bestseller lists and has been featured on "Fox & Friends" and "CNN American Morning." He participated on the "Good Morning America" Christmas Day panel in 2009 and 2010.

Randy Frazee co-hosted this special series that originated as a summer outreach program at Oak Hills Church. Many of the ideas for *Making Room for Neighbors* originated in his book *Making Room for Life* (Zondervan, 2003). In June 2008, Randy Frazee became the Senior Minister of Oak Hills Church in San Antonio, Texas, where he will teach and lead in partnership with pastor and author Max Lucado. Prior to coming to Oak Hills, he served as a Teaching Pastor at Willow Creek Community Church from 2005 to 2008. In addition to teaching, Randy oversaw Spiritual Development and a new neighborhood initiative at the church.

Prior to to his time at Willow Creek, Randy served as Senior Pastor at Pantego Bible Church in Fort Worth, Texas, for fifteen years. He is the author of *The Connecting Church*, *Making Room for Life*, and *Renovation of the Heart Student Edition*. An emerging leader and innovator in biblical community and spiritual formation, he has collaborated with George Gallup, Jr., on *The Christian Life Profile*, a spiritual assessment and development project.

A graduate of Dallas Theological Seminary, Frazee lives in the San Antonio area with his wife, Rozanne, and their four children and granddaughter.

SESSION TWO
Forgotten God

I've Got Jesus. Why Do I Need the Spirit?
by Francis Chan

Many people forget that God, the Holy Spirit, lives in every believer. Francis Chan, author of Crazy Love *and* Forgotten God, *challenges Christians at all stages of their walk with the extravagant and overwhelming truth of God's power in their lives. In this lesson from* Forgotten God, *a series on the Holy Spirit, Francis demonstrates the connection of the Holy Spirit to the growth and ministry of every believer.*

Where we think God is affects what we think about God. Maybe it shouldn't, but it certainly does. As we understand that God is present everywhere at all times, we should also understand that there is no place where we can't turn our thoughts toward God.

(For more information on the material in this session, read the Introduction and Chapter 1 of the book Forgotten God: Reversing Our Tragic Neglect of the Holy Spirit *by Francis Chan.)*

INTRODUCTION

Have you ever felt like you're missing something? Like you're getting by, but your life lacks something crucial, something extraordinary?

Somehow, we in the American church have managed to systematically neglect the power of the Holy Spirit. And the sad thing is that many people haven't even noticed. An increasing number of us recognize that there's a problem, but most of us still have no idea what we're missing out on.

In general, we don't value the Holy Spirit. But Jesus did: "It is the Spirit who gives life; the flesh is no help at all" (John 6:36 ESV). And from a biblical standpoint, you simply cannot live the Christian life without the Spirit of God. Paul says, "Anyone who does not have the Spirit of Christ does not belong to him" (Romans 8:9 ESV). We have no idea of the power available to us through the Spirit. Romans 8:11 tells us, "If the Spirit of him who raised Jesus from the dead dwells in you, he who raised Christ from the dead will also give life to your mortal bodies through his Spirit who dwells in you." Think of the power that it took to raise Jesus from the dead. Paul says that the same Holy Spirit who brings life out of death *lives inside us!*

How have we missed this? I'm guessing that you've heard these verses before. But most of us have probably come to accept our experience of the Christian life as normal. It's time to question what we've always thought. None of us is as biblical in our thinking as we'd like to believe.

Think about it for a minute. Why do you believe what you believe? What process do you follow in forming your beliefs? Most of us would probably say that our beliefs are based on the Word of God, but really, our beliefs are often born more out of convenience and consistency than careful study of the Scriptures. This is certainly true when it comes to our views about the Holy Spirit.

Chances are, you owe most of what you believe about the Holy Spirit to what you've seen and heard from the people around you. It's important to learn from other people, but at times we need to challenge our way of thinking. We are all in constant need of bringing our lives in line with the Scriptures.

1 Take a minute and list some of your beliefs about the Holy Spirit. (Even if you don't consider yourself a theologian, most of us have at least a few ideas about who the Holy Spirit is and what He does.)

_____
_____
_____
_____

2 Being as open as possible, do you think your beliefs are shaped more by the Scriptures or by what you've come to experience as the normal Christian life? What makes you say that?

_____
_____
_____
_____
_____

At some point, we all need to get past what we think we know about the Spirit. If we are going to rediscover the power and presence of the Holy Spirit, we will need to begin listening to His voice and following His leading—not in the ways we think He should speak and lead, but in whatever He may call us to do.

Roll Tape: DVD Session Two

DISCUSSION

In the busyness of our lives, we have developed a remarkable ability to miss the obvious. We overanalyze the things that don't deserve a second thought, and we blow right past the clear, obvious, important things in life.

We assume that we know what the Christian life ought to look like. But have you ever sat down and considered the way Scripture describes the Spirit-filled life?

1 The following passages offer a brief overview of what the Holy Spirit does in a person's life. Quickly flip through these passages and make some notes. (If you don't want to look up all of these passages, feel free to choose just a few at random.)

Acts 1:4–8

Acts 2:1–13

Acts 4:31

Romans 8:1–17

Romans 8:26–27

Romans 15:13

1 Corinthians 2:12–14

1 Corinthians 3:16

1 Corinthians 6:9–11

1 Corinthians 12:7–11

2 Corinthians 3:17–18

Galatians 4:4–7

Galatians 5:16–25

Ephesians 3:14–16

1 John 4:13

2 If you disregarded your own experiences and just read these passages, what would you expect to observe as the Holy Spirit entered a person's life?

_____
_____
_____
_____

3 For so many people in the church today, everyday life does not match these biblical descriptions. Why do you think that is?

_____
_____
_____
_____
_____

The statement is so familiar to us that we sometimes overlook its significance: "The Spirit of God dwells in you" (Romans 8:9 ESV). One obvious truth that we frequently overlook is that there should be a huge difference between someone who has the Spirit of God living inside of them and someone who does not.

Have you ever observed Christians and non-Christians interacting? In many cases, it is all but impossible to discern who has the Spirit and who doesn't. Sure, the Christians may be a little nicer or morally conscientious, but is that really *all* the Holy Spirit came to do in our lives? Shouldn't the difference be supernatural?

Read Galatians 5:16–25.

Paul is telling the Galatians what the Christian life ought to look like. In Christ, we have been set free from the law. But without the law, how do we please God? How do we love our neighbors as ourselves? For Paul, the answer is simple: Walk by the Spirit.

4 According to Galatians 5:16–25, what does it look like to walk by the Spirit?

_____
_____
_____
_____
_____

5 Based on what Paul says here, what should distinguish a Spirit-filled person from a non-Christian?

___

If the Holy Spirit is being neglected in our churches and in our lives, is it any wonder that we don't look much different from the rest of the world? Too often we work in our own strength to be the kind of people who stand out—the kind of people who look like Jesus. This is the right goal, but when we try to do this without relying on the Spirit, we're missing the whole point. Doesn't it strike you as odd that although we want to live out the attributes of Galatians 5:22–23, we don't rely on the Holy Spirit to produce the fruit *of the Spirit*?

Look at Galatians 5:16 again: "But I say, walk by the Spirit, and you will not gratify the desires of the flesh" (ESV). Perhaps we've gotten so caught up in trying to live the Christian life we've overlooked the Source. Life-change comes through the power of the Holy Spirit. At times we try so hard—but if we have forgotten about the Holy Spirit, then we're missing the whole point.

6 Every day, people try to live the "Spirit-filled" life without the Spirit. Based on your experience, what good things can we accomplish merely through human strength?

___

7 If the Spirit works through us, how should the supernatural results differ from what we can accomplish on our own?

___

I know that there are people in the church who live every day in the power of the Spirit, depending on and following Him in every aspect of life. Maybe you're one of those blessed few. Praise God if that's the case! But we all have room to grow. None of us has too much of the Spirit. We are all in danger of pursuing supernatural results through our own strength.

It's time for us to stop assuming that we know everything we need to know about the Holy Spirit. Some of us need to study a little deeper and find out who the Spirit is and what He does. This is an important step in the process. But all of us need to begin applying the obvious biblical truths about the Holy Spirit to our lives. Maybe you haven't missed the obvious doctrinally—maybe you've missed it practically. Until we actually apply the truth to our lives, we can't claim to believe it—at least not with any integrity.

Look again at the fruit of the Spirit listed in Galatians 5:22–23. Add to that list a host of other godly characteristics that we are called to pursue (such as faith, hope, compassion). These are not just abstract concepts. These fruits should be evident in our actions towards the people around us.

8 Don't just think about what the Holy Spirit can do for you. What are some clear and practical ways that the Spirit can work through you to bless the people around you?

_____

_____

_____

_____

Chapter 1 of the book *Forgotten God* ends with a powerful analogy about the confusion a caterpillar must experience:

> For all its caterpillar life, it crawls around a small patch of dirt and up and down a few plants. Then one day it takes a nap. And then, what in the world must go through its head when it wakes up to discover it can *fly*? What happened to its dirty, plump little worm body? What does it think when it sees its tiny new body and gorgeous wings?
>
> As believers, we ought to experience the same kind of astonishment when the Holy Spirit enters our bodies. We should be stunned in disbelief over becoming a "new creation" with the Spirit living in us. As the caterpillar finds its new ability to fly, we should be thrilled over our Spirit-empowered ability to live differently and faithfully. (*Forgotten God*, 37)

9 For all practical purposes, we seem to have forgotten that the Holy Spirit is powerful—He radically transforms lives. Are you open to being transformed, no matter what that may mean for your life? If you do want to be changed, why do you desire this? If you don't, what is keeping you from desiring change?

_____
_____
_____
_____

10 Spend some time praying that God will give you the humility to be open to what He wants to teach you—even if it means you've spent years overlooking the obvious. Then ask Him to begin using these truths to change the way you live.

_____
_____
_____
_____

REFLECTIONS ON ...
I've Got Jesus. Why Do I Need the Spirit?

_____
_____
_____
_____
_____
_____
_____
_____

MORE INFORMATION ABOUT THIS STUDY

This sample is the first session from the seven-session series *Forgotten God: Reversing Our Tragic Neglect of the Holy Spirit* by Francis Chan. The book by the same title, as well as the study guide and DVD, are published by David C. Cook Publishers and available online through Christian Book Distributors or at your local Christian bookstore.

Author

Francis Chan is the best-selling author of the books *Crazy Love*, *Forgotten God*, and *Erasing Hell* and is the host of the BASIC.series. He has also written the children's books *Halfway Herbert*, *The Big Red Tractor*, *The Little Village*, and *Ronnie Wilson's Gift*. Francis is the founding pastor of Cornerstone Church in Simi Valley, California, and is the founder of Eternity Bible College. He also sits on the board of directors of Children's Hunger Fund and World Impact. Francis now lives in northern California with his wife, Lisa, and their four daughters and one son.

SESSION THREE
Vintage Jesus

Is Jesus the Only God?
by Mark Driscoll

There are many opinions about Jesus. Every culture must include Jesus in some way. They certainly can't dismiss Him. But, in the context of culture, Jesus is presented as someone other than who He actually is.

What is the most serious decision a person can make about Jesus? Mark Driscoll will challenge you with the fact that what you decide about Jesus will affect every area of your life, both now and in the future. In this session, Mark will make the case for Jesus as God. Anything short of this view will lead to lives lived in contradiction to Scripture.

INTRODUCTION

Mark 14:61–62[*]

Again the high priest asked him, "Are you the Christ, the Son of the Blessed?" And Jesus said, "I am . . ."

This question has divided nations, incited political outrage and spawned centuries of theological debate and discourse. No question in life bears upon itself the weight of significance and responsibility that this one does. There are many questions that we can wrongly answer with varying degrees of consequences, but none is more important than this:

IS JESUS THE ONLY GOD?

There are a wide array of views concerning who the person of Jesus was in history and who He is today. Some say He was simply a great teacher, others say a prophet, while others suggest that He was merely a moral man who lived His life well, a worthy example of how we should in turn live our lives.

---

[*]All Scripture quotations in this session are taken from the English Standard Version.

While there are many views about who Jesus is, what role He played in history and what role He still plays today, no view is more important than the view Jesus had of Himself. His claims of being one with God the Father, having the power to perform miracles and forgive sin, living in a sinless state of perfection, sitting as the supreme authority over all creation and existing as God in eternity all demand a response on our part. Will we believe that He is who He claims to be? Or will we consider Him to be a lunatic who died a brutal death on the Cross for His commitment to a series of claims that were ultimately untrue?

In this session we will explore the different historical, social, and religious views of who Jesus is, as well as examine some of the claims that Jesus made of Himself as recorded in Scripture. We will then ask the question in response, *If Jesus is who He says He is, what difference does that make in my life?*

John 6:38

For I have come down from heaven, not to do my own will but the will of him who sent me.

John 10:32

Jesus answered them, "I have shown you many good works from the Father, for which of them are you going to stone me?"

John 8:46

Which one of you convicts me of sin? If I tell the truth, why do you not believe me?

Psalm 51:4

Against you, you only, have I sinned and done what is evil in your sight, so that you may be justified in your words and blameless in your judgment.

Luke 5:20–21

And when he saw their faith, he said, "Man, your sins are forgiven you." ²¹ And the scribes and the Pharisees began to question, saying, "Who is this who speaks blasphemies? Who can forgive sins but God alone?"

Mark 14:61b–64

Again the high priest asked him, "Are you the Christ, the Son of the Blessed?" ⁶² And Jesus said, "I am, and you will see the Son of Man seated at the right hand of Power, and coming with the clouds of heaven." ⁶³ And the high priest tore his garments and said, "What further witnesses do we need? ⁶⁴ You have heard his blasphemy . . ."

John 8:58–59

Jesus said to them, "Truly, truly, I say to you, before Abraham was, I am." ⁵⁹So they picked up stones to throw at him, but Jesus hid himself and went out of the temple.

John 10:30–33

"I and the Father are one." ³¹The Jews picked up stones again to stone him. ³²Jesus answered them, "I have shown you many good works from the Father; for which of them are you going to stone me?" ³³The Jews answered him, "It is not for a good work that we are going to stone you but for the blasphemy, because you, being a man, make yourself God."

Deuteronomy 6:4

Hear, O Israel: The Lord our God, the Lord is one.

Matthew 28:18

And Jesus came and said to them, "All authority in heaven and on earth has been given to me."

John 14:6

Jesus said to him, "I am the way, and the truth, and the life. No one comes to the Father except through me."

Roll Tape: DVD Session Three

DISCUSSION QUESTIONS

1 Do you believe that Jesus is the only God?

_____
_____
_____

There are a ton of questions that you can get wrong throughout life with varying degrees of pain and difficulty. This question, however, is the most important.

2 If so, why? Which reason is most compelling for you?

_____
_____
_____

3 In your opinion, why do people struggle to believe the claims that Jesus made about Himself?

_____
_____
_____

. . . within pop culture, Jesus is sort of a marketing item and in many ways is just a great example of a great person, but not widely believed to be God.

4 How do you see Jesus viewed in popular culture today?

_____
_____
_____

. . . Jesus clearly, emphatically, repeatedly said, "I am God."

5 Who do you need to speak with about Jesus, answering any questions he or she may have about Him?

_____
_____
_____

KEY THOUGHT

Everything hinges on whether or not you believe Jesus is God, including the quality of life that you live today and the eternity of life that you'll have after this life.

Prayer Requests

_____
_____
_____

Notes

MORE INFORMATION ABOUT THIS STUDY

This sample is the first session from the 12-session series *Vintage Jesus* by Mark Driscoll. The DVD teaching sessions are adapted from a sermon series at Mars Hill Church. The book *Vintage Jesus* by Mark Driscoll and Gerry Breshears is published by Crossway Publishers. The study series is published by Hudson Productions (2008). Both the book and DVD curriculum are available online through Christian Book Distributors or at your local Christian bookstore.

Author

Mark Driscoll is the founding pastor of Mars Hill Church, which started in 1996 as a small Bible study led by him and his wife, Grace, at their home in Seattle—the least churched city in America at the time. Since then, Mars Hill has been recognized as the 54th largest, 30th fastest-growing, and 2nd most innovative church in America by *Outreach* magazine and exploded with upwards of nineteen thousand people meeting across thirteen locations in four states.

Pastor Mark is one of the world's most downloaded and quoted pastors. He holds a B.A. in Speech Communication from Washington State University and a master's degree in Exegetical Theology from Western Seminary. He is the author of fifteen books, and the co-founder of the Acts 29 Network, which has planted over

400 churches in the US in addition to ministry in thirteen other nations. He also founded The Resurgence, which receives close to six million visits annually and services Christian leaders through books, blogs, conferences, and classes. Grace Driscoll delights in being a stay-at-home mom and helping raise the Driscolls' three sons and two daughters. She is also a graduate of the Edward R. Murrow School of Communication at Washington State University, where she earned a B.A. in Public Relations.

Find out more about Pastor Mark and Grace at www.PastorMark.tv.

SESSION FOUR
Not a Fan

Fan or Follower?
by Kyle Idleman

Kyle Idleman is a man on a mission. In a world that settles for casual or superficial interests, Kyle has decided to side with Jesus and insist on a life of commitment. Kyle shows in this session that becoming a follower of Jesus rather than just a fan is eventually going to be costly, perhaps in ways that will surprise you. Are you among the fans or the followers of Jesus?

If this is a new group or an existing group with new member(s) be sure to allow some time for everyone to introduce themselves (name tags are recommended in this case). Be sure to introduce yourself as well and explain to the group why you have chosen to lead this study.

INTRODUCTION

Write a prayer below for your group.

_____
_____
_____
_____

What are you really asking God to do?

_____
_____
_____
_____

OPENING QUESTIONS

-*What do you hope to get out of this study?*

-*What does the phrase "not a fan" mean to you?*

-*What does God want from you?*

Roll Tape: DVD Session Four

STORY CONTENT

Just curious, how do you feel after watching the first episode?

_____
_____
_____
_____

After hearing some reflections, read this: This is a pretty tough first lesson in the series. No patty-caking around. So we won't go light in our discussion, either. Oftentimes in Bible studies we ask theoretical questions, like "What do you think verse 3 means?" Or, "What is the most important thing a person should do?" There will be some hypothetical questions like that. But since fans typically like the theoretical questions because they keep the issues (and Jesus) at a comfortable distance, we will also ask questions of the personal, challenging kind. Like, "What is this verse saying about your life?" Or "What is the most important thing for you to do next?" These are questions followers love because answering helps them become better followers, and that is what true followers desire.

But let me add, no one has to answer any question. We don't want to force anything on anyone. Following Jesus is voluntary, so surely responding to the questions must be as well.

One other thing, this is a challenging study, but we also don't want this to be a place where we end up judging who is a follower and who is not. The quickest way to shut down the authenticity in this group is for us to start judging each other's lives. This study is not about making others to be better followers but about each of us individually challenging ourselves. So let's avoid any hint of judgment. Agreed? OK, good. Now before we ask some pointed questions, let's explore the story we've just watched.

Kyle is at a football game having a good time when he receives news of a friend's heart attack. At the hospital, he and the family receive word from the doctor that Eric Nelson has suffered irreversible brain damage. Everyone is shaken. If you have been in a situation like that, what was it like for everything to be normal one moment, then drastically different the next?

Kyle visits the grieving family and friends: Eric's wife Anna; and briefly, Eric's daughter Natalie and son Tony; his father Bill, and a couple of Eric's friends, Darren and Gary. How do you see the various characters reacting to death? How are these reactions like or different from what you have observed in similar situations?

GOING DEEPER

Let's turn to Luke 9:18–25.

Would someone be willing to read?

Oftentimes in these studies, the leader's guide asks the questions, but what questions come to your mind about this passage?

What stands out to you from this section of Scripture?

_____

_____

_____

_____

Notice the progression in the passage:

First, in vv. 18–21, Jesus is recognized as the Christ or Messiah of God. In another Gospel, Peter's confession includes the title, "Son of God."

Next, in v. 22, Jesus reveals that even though He is the Christ or actually because He is the Christ, He will suffer, die, and then rise again. If He is the anointed of God, why must He die?

Finally, in vv. 23–25, He tells his followers that they must die as well, die to themselves. But if they do, they too will be raised, their lives will be saved. Jesus adds, "If anyone tries to save his life, he will lose it." Why is this so? How does trying to save one's life lead to losing one's life?

PERSONAL CHALLENGE

When have you been most alive? Can you describe it?

_____
_____
_____
_____

Were you dead to yourself at the time or alive to yourself?

_____
_____
_____
_____

Think of a time when you were alive, and it was all about you—basically satisfying your own desires. *(Take a moment to come up with one.)* And a time when you were alive and it wasn't about you, but about others. *(Take a moment to come up with one.)*

Compare or contrast the two—how are they alike?

_____
_____
_____
_____

How are they different? Which do you prefer?

_____
_____
_____

Now some tougher questions. So, "Define the relationship."

How would you define what happens between you and Jesus? What terms would you use? Fan, follower, something else?

_____
_____
_____

How do you feel about your answer?

_____
_____
_____

To define the relationship implies you can have a real relationship with Jesus. How does a person have a relationship with Jesus, someone he can't see or touch? What is that like? How does it work for you?

What has following Jesus cost you?

_____
_____
_____

Do you feel like Jesus has tested your relationship with Him?

_____
_____
_____

If so, how? In what area(s)?

_____
_____
_____

If He were to test your relationship to Him these days, what might be a likely area? Something at work, home, in relationships, with money? What?

_____
_____
_____

Are there any areas of your life that are off-limits to Jesus?

_____
_____
_____

If so, why? What is your reason for keeping Him out? What has been the effect of keeping Him out?

_____

_____

If you suddenly died, and family and friends were asked for one thing about you, what do you believe they would say?

_____

_____

How do you feel about that? When you do actually die (at some, hopefully distant, point) what would you like people to say then?

_____

_____

What kind of life, what kind of changes or decisions, would it take in your life for people to actually make those kinds of comments about you at the time of your death?

_____

_____

That was a heavy lesson and some tough questions.

Thanks for hanging in there.

PRAYER TIME

What do you really hope for this group?

Use the space below to write your observations of the group and prayer concerns for the members.

_____
_____
_____
_____
_____
_____
_____
_____
_____
_____
_____
_____
_____

MORE INFORMATION ABOUT THIS STUDY

This sample is the first session from the six-session series *Not a Fan* by Kyle Idleman. The book, study guide, journal, and series are published by City on a Hill Studio and available online through Christian Book Distributors or at your local Christian bookstore.

Author

Kyle Idleman is the Teaching Pastor at Southeast Christian Church in Louisville, Kentucky, the 5th largest church in America, where he speaks to over 20,000 each weekend. He is the author and presenter of the award-winning video curriculum series *H2O: A Journey of Faith* as well as *The Easter Experience* and the *Not a Fan* book and DVD teaching series. Kyle is often invited as a guest speaker for regional and national conventions across the country and regularly speaks for some of America's most influential churches. He and his wife, DesiRae, have four young children.

SESSION FIVE
Life's Toughest Questions

Does God Care?
by Erwin McManus

Life throws problems at every person. Difficulties and disease, hardship and hard knocks will blindside everyone sooner or later. It rains on the just and the unjust alike. But where is God in the middle of your problems?

"Does God even care?" This is a tough question that comes from a tough place. When life hasn't worked out exactly like you think it should, it's tempting to question the goodness of God. In this session, you will be challenged to answer that question in both good times and bad.

INTRODUCTION

Asking the question, "Does God exist?" takes us into apologetic defenses, arguments, and the highest heights of philosophical reasoning. Many would say it is the most important question in the world. Yet could there be a question that is even more important?

The question, "Does God care?" has divided friends and family. The most brilliant men and women have debated it for thousands of years. It cuts to the heart of our view of the world in which we live. It shapes our view of ourselves. Like politics and education, it is a question nearly everyone has an opinion about and an opinion nearly every person cares about.

WARM UP

Try not to spend too much time here, but let everyone answer the warm-up questions. Getting group members involved early helps create the best small-group environment.

List five fictional characters—from movies, books, fairy tales, holidays. If these characters existed, how much would it affect your life on a day-to-day basis? How much would it affect your life when suffering came?

The information below sets up the video. It can be read aloud to the group, read by group members ahead of time, or group members can read the information silently while the facilitator sets up the video.

For the most part, whether or not Santa, Indiana Jones, or Uncle Scrooge exist doesn't affect our lives. This idea of Santa may impact our shopping habits once a year. Indiana Jones would have died several decades ago. And an old miser living in the 19th century doesn't really influence our Facebook® pages, gas prices, or relationships.

Some people feel the same way about God. They agree that maybe He does exist, but they don't necessarily believe His existence impacts them—much less that He cares about them.

Could this be the great dilemma of our souls? Not asking the intellectual question of whether or not He actually cares?

How might the realization that God cares change our lives and even heal our souls?

Take a moment to read the Scripture passages on page 41 before watching "Does God Care?" Then discuss the two questions designed as follow-up to the video in the Viewer Guide section.

Roll Tape: DVD Session Five

VIEWER GUIDE

Included are two questions designed as follow-up to "Does God Care?" This time is set aside for discussion within the group about what they heard, how it affected them, and possible applications. These questions may be only a beginning. Feel free to begin the conversation by asking what thoughts, insights, or stories had the most impact on group members.

> "It's one thing to come to know that God exists.
>
> It's another thing when you come to know that He cares."

1 Jesus doesn't always take away our pain—sometimes He leaves us in our loss. According to Erwin's message, what can we know to be true about God even in those times?

_____

_____

_____

_____

2 What is God's primary motivation? What evidence do we have of that?

_____

_____

_____

_____

BIBLICAL BACKGROUND

With music there is usually a story behind the song that helps listeners appreciate the heart and soul behind both the music and the lyrics. Scripture is no different. Below you'll find a brief story behind the week's Scripture intended to provide additional understanding and insight.

In the story of Lazarus, Jesus approaches the home of His deceased friend. In Jewish tradition, when someone died or some other tragedy occurred, people would often hire mourners to come and cry in order to create a sense of sorrow. The tears were real but the sorrow wasn't.

This is what made Jesus' tears so unique. When the onlookers expressed "See how He loved him!" (John 11:36 NIV) they were marveling about how Jesus' weeping wasn't just another paid performance; it was an honest expression.

The passage in Isaiah is prophetic literature. This type of literature has two general characteristics. The first is that it describes the future—probably the most common definition of "prophet." The second is that it calls people to create a better future. Martin Luther King, Jr., and Gandhi might be considered by some as prophets in this sense. All prophets in the Scriptures were both—they described the future as well as called the people of Israel to create a better future.

SCRIPTURE

Jesus wept. —John 11:35 (NIV)

¹⁹Everything God made is waiting with excitement for God to show his children's glory completely.... ²¹everything God made would be set free from ruin to have the freedom and glory that belong to God's children. —Romans 8:19, 21 (NCV)

¹Then I saw a new heaven and a new earth, ... ³And I heard a loud voice from the throne saying, "Now the dwelling of God is with men, and he will live with them. They will be his people, and God himself will be with them and be their God. ⁴He will wipe every tear from their eyes. There will be no more death or mourning or crying or pain, ... ⁵I [God] am making everything new!" —Revelation 21:1, 3–5 (NIV)

If anyone is in Christ, he is a new creation; the old has gone, the new has come!
—2 Corinthians 5:17 (NIV)

He was wounded for the wrong we did;
He was crushed for the evil we did.
The punishment, which made us well, was given to him,
And we are healed because of his wounds. —Isaiah 53:5 (NCV)

SMALL-GROUP QUESTIONS

Over the next few pages you'll find discussion questions, material that may be used as additional discussion points, and a journal exercise for group members to complete away from the group.

> "How many times in our lives have we been in a moment and we've cried out to God and it just seemed as if the universe was silent?"

1 Have you ever felt like God wasn't there when you needed Him? Or been with someone who searched for God in a time of pain and suffering but couldn't seem to find Him? Share an example.

_____
_____
_____
_____

2 How do you usually interact with God in times like you just shared?

___

"The first reason we suffer is it's self-inflicted, and we need to take responsibility for it. . . . There's enough food on this planet to feed every hungry person on this earth. We just don't want to."

___

3 What do you think it is about the human condition that makes it so easy to blame God for suffering instead of taking responsibility for the way we treat other people?

___

4 What are some excuses people give for not stepping up to help alleviate suffering in the world?

5 How do you think the consequences of our own decisions and influences (or lack of influence) can be reconciled with the fact that God is sovereign?

_____
_____
_____
_____

"Global warming. Cancer. Hurricanes. Disease. We didn't choose these things, but Scripture teaches that as humans disconnected from God, the world God originally created as good began to experience these consequences. Insurance agencies call them 'acts of God.' They are natural consequences of living in a fallen world."

6 Is it possible that God could be both immanent (near, indwelling) and eminent (high, unreachable)? Explain.

_____
_____
_____
_____

7 What is God's response when things happen to us that are outside of our control?

_____
_____
_____
_____

CHAOS THEORY

This theory, made famous by Ian Malcolm in the film *Jurassic Park* (1993), is a combination of physics, mathematics, and philosophy to explain the unpredictability of complex systems. The famed "butterfly effect" (for instance, the wings of a butterfly flapping in Brazil causing a hurricane in the Gulf of Mexico) shows the theoretical interconnectedness of every particle of matter in the universe.

Whether or not it's true that every action we take is connected to a series of actions and reactions of every other particle of matter in the universe, we know that the world is more complicated than we realize. It is more of a mystery than we realize. Yet our actions, and the actions of people who have lived over the course of human history, have had effects—both positive and negative—in ways that we will never fully understand.

> "[God] not only embraces our pain but He takes it upon Himself. And all the suffering, all the evil, all the wickedness, all the wounding He bore on Himself so that through His wounds all of us might be healed."

8 C. S. Lewis refers to this sacrifice, healing, and reconciliation as a "deeper magic." Reread the Scriptures on page 41 and discuss the ways God heals us.

_____
_____
_____
_____
_____

9 Do you think God is willing to step into your pain with you? Why or why not?

_____
_____
_____
_____

JOURNAL

This journaling opportunity is designed for group members to utilize at another time. They may choose to answer the question in the space provided or they may prefer to use the space and time to take a deep question or concern to God.

> "Our world is in disarray because our hearts are in disarray. And God is the One who's proactively intervening to diminish the destructive effect of our actions and to act with compassion and love so that we might find His healing in the midst of our suffering."

How does knowing and understanding more of the backstory of who God is, why He created us, and how He passionately loves us change your life and even heal your soul?

YOU'RE UP

As you think about connecting with God in your pain and joining with Him to alleviate the pain of others in the world, make time to do the following:

Examine instances when you have had a tendency to incorrectly place blame for the suffering in the world or your life. Ask God to show you His truth.

Ask God to use this week's Scripture passages to remind you of how much He cares.

Spend some time thinking about obstacles you might be putting up between you and God that get in the way of you experiencing His compassion and love.

Think of some ways you can take more initiative in alleviating the suffering of others.

MORE INFORMATION ABOUT THIS STUDY

This sample is the first session from the six-session series *Life's Toughest Questions* by Erwin McManus, part of the Platform Series published by LifeWay Publishers and is available from LifeWay online and in their local stores. The teaching is adapted from the speaking ministry of Erwin McManus.

Author

Erwin Raphael McManus is an author, speaker, activist, filmmaker, and innovator who specializes in the field of developing and unleashing personal and organizational creativity, uniqueness, innovation, and diversity. In other words, he gets bored really easily. He is committed to creating environments that expand imagination, unleash creativity, and maximize the creative potential in every individual and organization. Erwin is also the catalyst behind Awaken. Convinced that the world is changed by dreamers and visionaries, Awaken serves the purpose of history by maximizing the divine potential in every human being.

Erwin is the architect of Mosaic in Los Angeles. He is the author of *An Unstoppable Force*, a Gold Medallion Award finalist, as well as *Chasing Daylight*, *Uprising: A Revolution of the Soul*, *The Barbarian Way*, *Stand Against the Wind*, *Soul Cravings*, and *Wide Awake*. He also serves as a Research Advisor with The Gallup Organization.

Erwin is a native of El Salvador, and is a graduate of the University of North Carolina and Southwestern Theological Seminary. He and his wife, Kim, live in Los Angeles and have two children, Aaron and Mariah, and a foster daughter Paty.

SESSION SIX
When I Don't Desire God

The Fight for Joy Is Essential (Part 1)
by John Piper

Early in his ministry, John Piper discovered that every page of the Bible reveals the glory of God and the fact that we are created first and foremost to the glory of God Himself. The term that best describes the kind of people God wants us to be is a "Christian hedonist."

This session will challenge you to think about your relationship with God in a different way. John Piper helps us reframe that relationship with language of delight rather than duty. You will discover what God has to do with joy no matter what else is happening in your life.

LESSON OBJECTIVES

It is our prayer that after you have finished this lesson . . .

- You will discover how you and others in your group view the role of joy in the Christian life.
- Your curiosity would be roused, and questions would begin to come to mind.
- You will be eager to learn more about how you can fight for joy in God.

ABOUT YOURSELF

1 What is your name?

_____

2 Tell the group something about yourself that they probably don't already know.

_____

_____

_____

3 Describe your relationship with Jesus.

Roll Tape: DVD Session Six

A PREVIEW OF *WHEN I DON'T DESIRE GOD*

1 In your mind, is the fight for joy essential to the Christian life? What strategies do you use in your fight for joy?

2 In the space below, describe the current state of your relationship with Christ. What are the most significant obstacles to deeper fellowship with God? How are you seeking to overcome these obstacles? Be specific.

MORE INFORMATION ABOUT THIS STUDY

This sample is the first session from the eight-session series *When I Don't Desire God* by John Piper. The book with the same title and study series are published by Crossway Books and available online through Christian Book Distributors or at your local Christian bookstore.

Author

John Piper, who is the Pastor for Preaching at Bethlehem Baptist Church in Minneapolis, Minnesota. He grew up in Greenville, South Carolina, and studied at Wheaton College, where he first sensed God's call to enter the ministry. He went on to earn degrees from Fuller Theological Seminary (B.D.) and the University of Munich (D.theol.). For six years he taught Biblical Studies at Bethel College in St. Paul, Minnesota, and in 1980 accepted the call to serve as pastor at Bethlehem. John is the author of more than thirty books, and more than twenty-five years of his preaching and teaching are available for free at www.desiringGod.org. John and his wife, Noel, have four sons, one daughter, and an increasing number of grandchildren.

SESSION SEVEN
Guarding Your Child's Heart

Do You Have a Plan?
by Gary Smalley

Guarding your child's heart doesn't happen accidentally. We need a strategy that has proven effective in helping children grow into healthy, mature adults. Gary Smalley helps guide parents into how to do this with confidence.

Often parents plan ahead for their child's future in the event of their death or some other emergency. But how do you create a plan for a child's life? Where do you want to see your child go? What do you want to see your child grow to become? Gary gives powerful insights into creating such a plan.

GETTING STARTED
Read Ephesians 6:10–13:

> *Finally, be strong in the Lord and in his mighty power. Put on the full armor of God so that you can take your stand against the devil's schemes. For our struggle is not against flesh and blood but against the ruler, against the authorities, against the powers of this dark world and against the spiritual forces of evil in the heavenly realms. Therefore put on the full armor of God, so that when the day of evil comes, you may be able to stand your ground, and after you have done everything, to stand.* (NIV)

How does this passage relate to Ephesians 6:1–4?

_____
_____
_____
_____

What are a few ways the Enemy has attacked your home?

_____
_____
_____

How have you prepared your children for the attacks of Satan? Do you have a written plan to protect your children from the attacks of Satan?

_____
_____
_____

Roll Tape: DVD Session Seven

SESSION INTRODUCTION

There is an Enemy who wants to destroy your home. His crosshairs are on your children. He has four very powerful and destructive beliefs that he wants you and your children to hide within your heart. These four toxic beliefs are explored in later sessions of *Guarding Your Child's Heart*. As you look around to what is happening in our world of crime and evil, most of the destruction and negative actions come directly from Satan's four toxic beliefs lodged within mankind's hearts. Since he is the chief liar, he wants to steal your heart away from all that is good, kill everything honorable within you and your children, destroying your marriage, family, and lives (see John 10:10).

But Christ came to bring you and your children abundant, overflowing life. He wants you to have amazing freedom from everything evil and establish within your heart four powerful beliefs that lead to a blessed life here and eternal life forever.

I can honestly admit to you that I've never been happier in my entire life than I am today. I want to follow all of the 131 teachings of Christ; but to start, I've embraced four of Christ's powerful teachings that alone have enriched me more than I could have ever imagined. I'm even learning how to fit all 131 of Christ's commands into the four that I use every day!

With Satan's clever lying ways, no wonder there is so much crime and destruction in our world today. But, just imagine how many evil and negative thoughts were in the hearts of those who destroyed the World Trade Center? This giant example of evil on September 11, 2001, caught America off guard. We were not prepared. We did not have the enemy sized up properly. Look at these words from *The 9/11 Commission Report*:

> We learned about an enemy who is sophisticated, patient, disciplined, and lethal. The enemy rallies broad support in the Arab and Muslim world by demanding redress of political grievances, but its hostility toward us and our values is limitless. Its purpose is to rid the world of religious and political pluralism, the plebiscite, and equal rights for women. It makes no distinction between military and civilian targets. **Collateral damage** is not in its lexicon.
>
> We learned that the institutions charged with protecting our borders, civil aviation, and national security did not understand how grave this threat could be, and did not adjust their policies, plans, and practices to deter or defeat it . . .
>
> The test before us is to sustain that unity of purpose and meet the challenges now confronting us.
>
> We need to design a balanced strategy for the long haul, to attack terrorists and prevent their ranks from swelling while at the same time protecting our country against future attacks.

This report is the best commentary on Ephesians 6:10–13 that I have ever read.

> Finally, be strong in the Lord and in his mighty power. Put on the full armor of God so that you can take your stand again the devil's schemes. For our struggle is not against flesh and blood, but against the rulers, against the authorities, against the powers of this dark world and against the spiritual forces of evil in the heavenly realms. Therefore put on the full armor of God, so that when the day of evil comes, you may be able to stand your ground, and after you have done everything, to stand. (NIV)

Satan is sophisticated, patient, disciplined and lethal. He hates your family. He will utilize everything in his arsenal to destroy your marriage and your children. His strategy is to ruin not only your marriage, but also the future marriages of your children.

We must understand how grave this threat really is. We have been given the armor of God to protect our hearts. It is not an accident that Ephesians 6:10–13 follows the Bible's central teaching on marriage and family in Ephesians 5:22–6:4. The test before us is to sustain the unity of purpose and meet the challenges now confronting us. We need to design a balanced strategy for the long haul, to put on the full armor of God and prevent Satan from having victory in his future attacks.

Is your home prepared for the attacks of the Enemy? Do you have a plan to guard your child's heart from the impending attacks of Satan?

PARENT POINT

Every parent needs a deliberate, strategic, and measurable plan to guard his or her child's heart.

GUARDING THE PARENT'S HEART

For years you have been imparting thoughts and beliefs to your child's heart that actually come from your own heart. Were you raised in a home with no guarding plan, and now you may be continuing the negative cycle? Here's the great news: You can break any negative, toxic cycle. I did. My father was a very angry man. I made the decision early on in my marriage and family to break the cycle of anger. Why? Because my children get the overflow of my heart. Many of you grew up hearing your parents make statements such as,

- You'd better change your tune pretty quick.
- You act as though the world owes you something.
- You've got a chip on your shoulder.
- You're not going anywhere looking like that.
- I never saw a kid like you.
- Other kids don't try stuff like that.
- I wasn't like that.
- Why can't you be more like your brother/sister?
- I'm your father/mother; as long as you live in my house, you'll do as I say.
- Are you going to apologize to me? Well, "sorry" is just not good enough!
- If I've told you once, I've told you a thousand times.
- We're going to church and when we get there I want you to act like a Christian.

If you've never learned how to guard your own heart, that's where we will start.

Then, just think of how many hours you and your children have been bombarded with the lies of this world through TV, movies, music, magazines, school teachers, friends, and the list goes on and on.

What messages have been written on your heart? Do you know what negative belief is behind them?

_____
_____
_____

Name a few things your parents said to you on a regular basis that were positive.

_____
_____
_____

Name a few things your parents said to you on a regular basis that were negative.

_____
_____
_____

What statements from your childhood are you repeating to your children?

_____
_____
_____

RED BELIEFS VERSUS PURPLE BELIEFS

Solomon said to "guard your heart, for it is the wellspring of life" (Proverbs 4:23 NIV). Your heart is shaped by what you think about all day long. And you alone get to choose what you think about every day.

You can either live in the negative or live in the positive. You can dwell on negative feelings and thoughts of anger, resentment, and get-even tactics. Or you can take the words of the apostle Paul when he said, "Whatever is true, whatever is noble, whatever is right, whatever is pure, whatever is lovely, whatever is admirable—if anything is excellent or praiseworthy—*think* about such things" (Philippians 4:8 NIV, emphasis added).

You have two choices. One, you can think like Christ (as in Philippians 4:8). We will be referring to these as **Red Beliefs** throughout this study. Or, you can think like the prince of the world (negative). We will be referring to these as **Purple Beliefs** throughout this study.

You'll have thousands of thoughts every day whether you like it or not. Which would you rather have? Thoughts controlled by the world and the prince of this world or thoughts controlled by God, filled with love and desire to care for people?

FOUR KEY BELIEFS FROM SCRIPTURE

The beliefs of your heart usually come from your parents, or you may pick them up from culture. Thus we are likely to be as happy or unhappy as our parents were or as our culture is as a whole. But I don't want my happiness to be dependent on others, whether it's my parents or the culture in general. I know that God created me to be filled with joy, peace, and love, and therefore, I have found the four major beliefs I am basing my life on today. These four beliefs will become the foundation for the plan you and your children can develop throughout this study. These are the key beliefs I have been diligent to embed, or hide, in my heart so that they become guiding principles for everything I do in life. And I have found that they work. If we will conform our minds to these four key beliefs that were designed by our Maker, they will put us on top of everything that matters in life.

These four beliefs need to be established firmly in your life so they can in turn be included in your plan and impressed on the hearts of your children. Here is just a brief outline of these four beliefs:

1 **Humble Yourself.** You are promised by Jesus that if you humble yourself before God and think of yourself as a helpless person or as a beggar, unable on your own to create His type of love and power, you will become "poor in Spirit." Then, as this sense of powerlessness grows into a huge belief within your heart, He will give you the kingdom of heaven as a reward today and forever (see Matthew 5:3; James 4:6).

2 **Love God.** If you humble yourself before God and cry out as a beggar for His love and power, He'll reward you so that you in turn can use His love and power to love God with all your heart, soul, mind, and strength (see Deuteronomy 6:5; Matthew 22:37).

3 **Love Others.** If you remain humble before God and cry out as a beggar for His love and power, He'll reward you so that you in turn can use His love and power to love others as you love yourself (see Galatians 5:14).

4 **Rejoice in Trials.** If you remain humble before God and cry out as a beggar for His love and power, He'll reward you so that you in turn can use His love and power to give thanks to Him and even rejoice during *all* circumstances, good and bad (see Romans 5:3–5; James 1:2–4).

I'm seventy years old and more excited about today and what the future brings than at any other time in my life. I live with great hope about today and tomorrow. What will He inspire me to do today? Help someone I don't even know? Grant forgiveness to someone? Use me to bring others to Him? How will He use me tomorrow? Even the littlest things I do can be used mightily by God. All things are possible through Him (see Matthew 19:26). I get to discover His dreams for me and what He wants to do through me.

Nothing has changed my life more than these four beliefs. As I review and *think on* the Bible verses that support these four beliefs every day, my friends and family are finding that I complain less and serve more. I'm headed for a life of taking no credit. It is the power of God working through my spiritual journey. I find that I am overflowing each day and want to give more and more to Norma, my wife, on her spiritual journey. After all, I cannot give what I do not already have.

The result of embedding these four beliefs in my heart has been almost a complete victory over worry, judging others, irritation, lust, unhealthy eating habits, anger, complaining, disharmony with others, and ingratitude. My stress level is now almost nonexistent. My health is much better than it has been since I was a very young man. My blood pressure is 115/70, and that's after a heart attack. But even if my health fails and chronic aches and pains begin to wrack me, I will still be able to maintain a grateful heart and remain joyful—all because of these beliefs I have implanted in my heart and God's loving power.

Learn these principles and you will reap the wonderful consequences of a much closer walk with God and harmony with others. You'll be thrilled at the growing compassion in your heart toward all people. It all comes as a gift from God when you learn to adjust your deepest beliefs to only a few of the most powerful living words from Scripture. Just think of it, God's Word is Truth (see John 17:17), and you will know this truth, and it will set you free (see John 8:32).

You may be way beyond me in this journey. You may already have these four beliefs firmly hidden in your own heart. If so, that's great. For you, this study may be just a testimony of a person who is excitedly learning to walk with God and take His words and beliefs seriously. If you already know and live by these principles, you will be able to influence your children so that these amazing beliefs can be spread throughout the world.

PARENT PLAN

Acknowledge where you are with a plan for guarding your child's heart:

- We do not have a plan.
- We *have* a plan, but it needs some work.
- We have a solid plan for guarding our child's heart.

Do you believe that Satan has a battle plan for your home? List some ways you've seen the Enemy's plan work in your family.

_____

_____

_____

_____

_____

Do not let this catch you off guard. Be prepared with your own plan to guard the hearts of your family.

_____

_____

_____

_____

MEMORIZING SCRIPTURE

In this session, you'll have Scripture passages for memorization. I will offer a few passages; choose one for your family to memorize. If you're studying one session a week, you have a week to memorize and meditate on that Scripture. You can always take longer if needed. I'm asking you and your family to start with the four Beliefs and find verses that teach them. You might find a number of verses that match. We'll offer some suggested verses at the end of each session. Memorize the ones that light you up the most.

You can customize the verses according to the ages and needs of your children. A younger child may be able to learn one phrase or sentence. An older child can learn a longer passage. Teach them just enough that they can grasp the meaning and meditate on it each day.

Be sure this isn't a forced, negative situation for your kids. Find creative ways to make it fun. Here are some tips about times and ways to help your family memorize:

- While in traffic
- While exercising, running, or walking
- While waiting in lines
- At meals
- While getting ready in the morning
- At bedtime
- By tying the verse to a song or dance
- Sitting in my chair watching TV and memorizing during commercials
- During any boring times I face each week
- Rewarding your children when they finish memorizing

MEMORIZE AND MEDITATE

Above all else, guard your heart, for it is the wellspring of life. (Proverbs 4:23 NIV)

I have hidden your word in my heart that I might not sin against you. (Psalm 119:11 NIV)

Children, obey your parents in the Lord, for this is right. "Honor your father and mother"—which is the first commandment with a promise—"that it may go well with you and that you may enjoy long life on the earth." Fathers, do not exasperate [create anger in] your children; instead, bring them up in the training and instruction of the Lord. (Ephesians 6:1–4 NIV)

Finally, be strong in the Lord and in his mighty power. Put on the full armor of God so that you can take your stand against the devil's schemes. For our struggle is not against flesh and blood, but against the rulers, against the authorities, against the powers of this dark world and against the spiritual forces of evil in the heavenly realms. Therefore put on the full armor of God, so that when the day of evil comes, you may be able to stand your ground, and after you have done everything, to stand. (Ephesians 6:10–13 NIV)

MORE INFORMATION ABOUT THIS STUDY

This sample is the first session from the twelve-session series *Guarding Your Child's Heart* by Gary Smalley. The study guides and series are published by NavPress and available online through Christian Book Distributors or at your local Christian bookstore.

Author

Gary Smalley has become one of the country's best-known authors and speakers on family relationships. He is the author and co-author of twenty-eight best-selling, award-winning books along with several popular films and videos. He has spent over thirty-five years learning, teaching, and counseling. Gary has personally interviewed hundreds of singles and couples and has surveyed thousands of people at his seminars asking two questions: What is it that strengthens your relationships and what weakens them? Gary's twenty-eight books combined have sold over 6 million copies.

SESSION EIGHT
DO Something!

The Plan
by Miles McPherson

Miles McPherson, pastor of the Rock Church in San Diego, California, urges believers to just do something, as the title exclaims. Rather than viewing his weekend services as a safe haven for Christians, Miles wants to launch his church into the world. He wants every believer to make a difference and not just play it safe.

Miles shares a game plan for every believer. This lesson lays out an overview of God's plan for each believer's life as well as a pattern for this entire study of the things God wants to do in you, so He can get you to a place where He can work through you.

ORIENTATION AND OVERVIEW

The goal of this week's study is for members of the group to get acquainted, to talk about the basics of the session format, and to move into the *DO Something!* Experience.

For groups who choose to divide Week 1 into two weeks, the first week—Zero Week—includes the Orientation and ends with a potluck or meal.

Orientation Zero Week*

Getting to Know Your Group (10 min.)
- Take a few minutes to get to know each other.

---

*In the full study, there is the option to do the first session of DO Something! in 1 or 2 weeks. If your meetings are shorter than 1½ hours we encourage you to either break this into two weeks to get the full effect, or just go to the "An Overview of the 5 P's" section on page 63 and begin from there. The "Zero Week" material is an overview of the structure of the studies and can be omitted while still having a great experience with the "Week One" material.

Introduction to the *DO Something!* Experience (10 min.)

- Watch the welcome message from Miles McPherson.

What is the Ultimate Goal of the Group? (5 min.)

1 Become a *DO Something!* believer who is actively engaged in doing something obedient to God as an individual.

2 Become part of the solution to one of your community's problems. Join or start a ministry designed to bring Christ's love to your broken world.

Format of Weekly Sessions (10 min.)

After a review of the previous week's material, the core of the meeting covers eight steps. The following is a description of each step.

TEACHING

Participants will watch a DVD teaching from Miles McPherson while completing these four steps:

Step 1—God's Perspective

In Step 1 you will learn God's perspective on your life. God's perspective of your life is based on His unconditional love for you and His plans to use you to do great things in the world. The DVD teaching will guide everyone through the fill-in-the-blank questions about the lesson's topic.

Step 2—Our Brokenness

You will then skip down to Step 2 and look at your brokenness. Because of our brokenness, we have a very distorted view of our lives. We simply do not see ourselves like God does, and it's important for us to understand the extent to which our brokenness influences our decisions. The DVD teaching will guide everyone through the fill-in-the-blank questions about how our brokenness affects our perspective.

Step 3—Intersection

Step 3 lies in between the circles for Steps 1 and 2. Ministry happens when our brokenness intersects with and is submitted to God's ideal perspective for our lives. It is then that we must make a decision to do something to submit ourselves to His plan for our lives. The DVD teaching will guide everyone through the fill-in-the-blank questions about the lesson's topic.

Step 4—Do Something

Once you experience what God wants to do *in* you, you are ready for Him to do something *through* you. In Step 4 you will learn about applying your internal "do something" to help someone else in his or her time of need. Ministry happens when you apply the changes that God has made in your life to help someone else.

DISCUSSION

After viewing the DVD teaching, a group discussion follows the same four steps. This is your opportunity to internalize the lesson and discuss how it applies to you.

Step 5—God's Perspective

Discuss what you've learned about God's perspective on your life.

Step 6—Our Brokenness

Discuss how your brokenness can distract you from God's perspective on His plan in your life.

Step 7—Intersection—Next Steps Preview

Now that you have learned two opposing views—God's perspective and how you view life through your brokenness—it is time to discuss what you need to allow God to do in your life to bring about His desired change. Keep in mind: what God does *in you* is going to lead to His doing something *through you*. This step will help prepare you for Step 8 and the practical *Do Something* Next Steps that you will complete during the week.

Step 8—Do Something—Next Steps Preview

The last discussion will prepare you to practically apply what you have learned and experienced to help someone who is in need.

You will have three *Do Something* Next Steps options. Each step builds on the previous one, starting with something simple in the first step. *Do only what you feel comfortable doing.*

> **Crawl**—This will usually be something simple you can do alone and most often contains a form of planning.
>
> **Walk**—This step is a little more aggressive *do something* and usually involves contacting someone via email, phone, or letter.

Run—This step will usually involve making personal contact with someone.

Each week you will be encouraged to bring back a report on what you did.

You'll also be asked to find an accountability partner to help you stay on track as you work through this study.

NOTE: *"(Optional)"* is placed next to questions you can respond to as time allows.

DO SOMETHING NEXT STEPS

The *Do Something* Next Steps are what you are responsible to do on your own outside the group meeting. These pages are designed to guide you through what you have been challenged to do in Step 8 of the week's lesson. You can also use these pages as a journal to record what happens.

Prayer (Zero Week Only)

Break (Zero Week: Potluck — Week 1: Short Break)

Use this snack or meal time to complete the sign-up sheets for contact information, refreshments, and child care as your group leader requests.

An Overview of the 5 P's (Week 1)
- Preparation: Advance Work
- Purpose: Obedience
- Pain: It Doesn't Have to Only Hurt
- Power: The Ability to Do
- Passion: Never Give Up

    God's plan for Jesus' life is the plan for *your* life too.

    Most assuredly, I say to you, he who believes in Me, the works that I do he will do also; and greater works than these he will do, because I go to My Father. —John 14:12 (NKJV)

According to Jesus, you were created to do something great!

Prayer Time (10 minutes)

Dear Lord, thank You for Your plan for our lives. We want to do something great. Jesus, we believe that You love us and will do great works through us. Please help us understand exactly what we need to do to fulfill our role in Your plan. In Jesus' name we pray, Amen.

Icebreaker (10 minutes)

Think about a time when you had a part in making a plan come together successfully—whether with your friends and family (party, reunion, trip); with your church (event, service project); at work (project, meeting); or elsewhere. What did you find most fulfilling about this experience?

BIBLE STORY: THURSDAY NIGHT—JOHN 14:12

Roll Tape: DVD Session Eight

PART 1: TEACHING (10 MINUTES)

Watch the session *DO Something!* on DVD 2 and fill in the blanks in the circles on pages 66–69.

PART 2: DISCUSSION (45 MINUTES)

Read John 14:12 together. Describe what you think it means to be able to do greater things than Christ.

Group Prayer (5 minutes)

Dear Lord, we know that You have a plan to put us in a position to do something great through our lives. We ask that You reveal Your plan to us each day. Please give us the faith to allow You to lead us through that plan.

NOTES

_____
_____
_____
_____
_____
_____
_____
_____
_____
_____
_____
_____
_____

PART 3: DO SOMETHING NEXT STEPS

God must do something in me before
He can do something through me.

Of all the P's, the one that scares me the most is _____

because _____

The biggest internal obstacle I will need to overcome is _____
_____
_____

Explain why it has been so hard to overcome. _____
_____
_____
_____

1. GOD'S PERSPECTIVE

1. God has a plan for you to do greater works than Him. *John 14:12*

2. You have been completely _____ to do something great. *Ephesians 2:10*

3. There is a simple _____ behind everything you do. *1 John 5:3*

4. What we will do will sometimes involve _____. *James 4:1-3*

5. God has provided _____ for you to do something. *Ephesians 3:20*

6. Doing something significant will require a passion that screams "Don't Quit!" *Luke 9:62*

3. INTERSECTION

God wants to do something *in* you.

1. _____ that God has a plan for your life.
2. _____ yourself to God's plan for your life.

2. OUR BROKENNESS

Because of our brokenness, we *CAN'T* accept or submit to His plan.

1. We lack the **C**_____ that God's plan is really the best thing for us.

2. We resist **A**_____ in our lives. We want to do our own thing. *Proverbs 10:17*

3. We are blind to the fact that God is **N**_____ us every step of the way.

4. We don't **T**_____ that He will be here for us through thick and thin.

4. DO SOMETHING

God wants to do something *through* you.

1. God's plan is designed to do something to you and then do something through you.
2. Whatever God does _____ you is always for the benefit of someone with a specific need.
3. Acknowledge that there are people _____ who will benefit from your fulfilling God's plan in your life.

5. GOD'S PERSPECTIVE

1. God has a plan to do something through your life on behalf of someone else. If you let go of all of the nervousness, doubt, fear, and excuses, what type of help do you think you would really enjoy providing for people?
2. Is there a specific group of people you feel God has planned for you to help? Why do you feel that?
3. Knowing that God has a plan for your life, how does that knowledge impact your decision-making process in your daily life? Give a specific example.

7. INTERSECTION

1. After hearing a brief overview of the five P's, which do you think is the hardest for you to fully embrace? Why? Describe the obstacle that will be first to get in your way.
2. If you could lean on the help of one person to encourage you through this process, who would it be?

6. OUR BROKENNESS

1. Describe a time you were a part of something that you believed in but that lacked leadership, organization, and vision. How did you react? How did this make you feel? How did it impact your participation?
2. In what ways have you had a similar attitude towards God and His plan?
3. (Optional) Is there a part of you that doubts that God has a plan? Why?

8. DO SOMETHING—next steps preview

Remember, Jesus said that if you believe in Him, you would do greater things than He did (*John 14:12*).

As a group, review these Next Step options:

1. **Crawl:** Begin a journal describing the kind of person you think you could become if God were to refine His plan in your life. For example, what behaviors and attitudes would be different? What fears would you need to overcome? What new disciplines would you need to begin? Dream big!

2. **Walk:** Describe the type of person you would like to become and identify someone you want to help if God's plan was fulfilled in your life. What changes in behavior or perspective would result in that person as a result of you doing something for them?

3. **Run:** Identify and explore a community organization or ministry that provides the kind of help God has created you to provide. Gather information on how they do what they do and why. Join them!

Accountability Partner

I will find an accountability partner by _____ (Date).

Suggested approach when asking someone to be an accountability partner:

> "How are you? First let me say I have great respect for you and your faith in God. I have a desire to grow in my relationship with God and I would like you to hold me accountable to meeting certain deadlines I will be setting for myself. As part of the weekly Bible study that I am a part of, I would like to ask that you be the person who signs off on my assignments. This will help me to be faithful to complete them and ensure that I put myself in the best position to grow spiritually."

My accountability partner is _____

God has a plan to do something

through me for someone.

Dream Big!

Crawl

If God were to refine His plan in my life . . .

- What behaviors, internal and external, would be different?

_____

_____

- What fears would I like to overcome?

_____

_____

- What new disciplines would I begin?

_____

_____

- How would this change the person I am?

_____

_____

Walk

Describe the type of help you would like to provide to someone by completing this sentence:

- I would like to help someone who is struggling with . . .

_____

_____

- After I help them, I would like them to be able to . . .

_____

_____

Run

Within the next _____ days, I am going to visit a _____ (community organization or ministry)

- While at this organization/ministry, I learned that God wants to use me to

_____

_____

- Based on what I did this week, what did God show me about myself?

_____

_____

- What did God show me about Himself?

_____

_____

Week 1 completed _____ (Date)

Accountability partner's signature:_____

PRAYER

Dear Lord, I know that You have a plan to put me in a position to do something great through my life. I ask that You reveal Your plan to me each day. Please give me the faith to allow You to lead me through that plan.

PREPARATION FOR NEXT WEEK

Make notes on your calendar for those items you have signed up to do at group.

MORE INFORMATION ABOUT THIS STUDY

This sample is the first session from the six-session series *DO Something!* by Miles McPherson. The book, study guides, and series are published by Baker Books and available online through Christian Book Distributors or at your local Christian bookstore.

Author

Miles McPherson, author of *Do Something! Make Your Life Count,* is a man who has been radically transformed by God. Miles is the Senior Pastor of the Rock Church in San Diego, one of the fastest-growing churches in the United States. A former defensive back with the San Diego Chargers, Miles is now the president and founder of Miles Ahead, an outreach ministry focused on sharing the good news of Jesus Christ with teens and adults all over the world. His newest book is *Do Something! Make Your Life Count.* Check out www.DoSomethingWorld.org to find out more about the DO Something World project and its opportunities. Two years into his professional football career, Miles was battling a drug problem and living an immoral lifestyle. That's when he gave his life to Jesus Christ, and never looked back. Miles began to work as a Bible teacher, youth pastor, and speaker with a track record of appealing to diverse audiences. Known for his frank and funny delivery, Miles loves to call people to think about how God has prepared them to do something significant with their lives. He's a prolific speaker, one who can talk to anyone from prison inmates to senior citizens. He challenges everyone to go out and do something for God!

SESSION NINE
Heaven

What We Know about Heaven
by Randy Alcorn

(Note: This session is meant to be a companion study to *Heaven* (Tyndale) and *50 Days of Heaven* (Tyndale). If the leaders have copies of those books, they'll be able to use the references that go with the discussion questions.)

Having devoted a good portion of his ministry to the study of Heaven, Randy Alcorn gives insights into something every believer thinks about on a regular basis. Even those who might doubt there is a god, hope there is a heaven. This lesson will help you unpack what the Bible says about where believers will spend eternity.

Heaven shouldn't be a vague and uncertain idea. God has revealed a great deal about Heaven through the Bible. But, we have many questions like "Who goes to Heaven?" or even "What about dogs?" Randy shares the biblical concept of Heaven and serves to answer questions like these.

INTRODUCTION

We want to welcome you to this exciting study on Heaven. Our prayer for you is to experience the reality of God in a way that really begins to transform your everyday life. God created each of us for a life that is far better than we ever imagined possible, and we want to do all that we can to embrace what He has for us.

As you join us on this journey, we hope you will personally encounter God in a profound way. And as you learn and grow, we hope you will share with others what you are learning. We are very excited that you have decided to join us in this study of Heaven.

In the video for this study on Heaven, Randy Alcorn discusses a renewed perspective of Heaven based on the reality of the present Heaven, the restoration promised in a New Earth, and the rewards of reigning and ruling with God on the New Earth, Eden reclaimed.

There are three phases: life on earth as we now know it, an Intermediate Heaven—the place we go when we die, and the New Heaven and New Earth we will inhabit after the resurrection. These three phases are depicted in the timeline below.

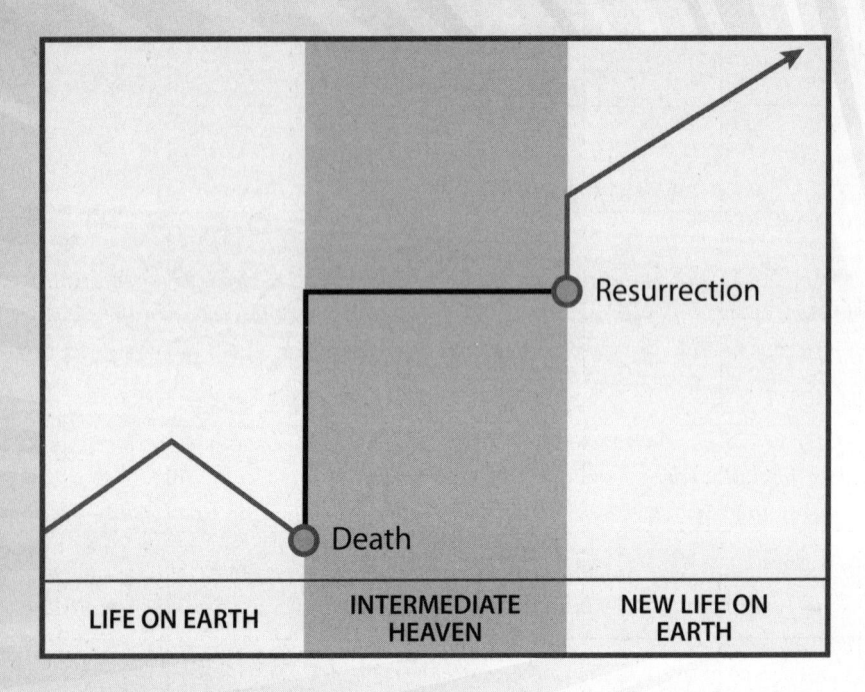

Timeline showing three phases: LIFE ON EARTH, INTERMEDIATE HEAVEN (beginning at Death), and NEW LIFE ON EARTH (beginning at Resurrection).

Memory Verse: *And I saw the holy city, the new Jerusalem, coming down from God out of heaven like a bride beautifully dressed for her husband. I heard a loud shout from the throne, saying, "Look, God's home is now among his people! He will live with them, and they will be his people. God himself will be with them."* (Revelation 21:2–3 [NLT])

Many people don't look forward to Heaven because it is a realm that we lack the ability to see or easily understand. We are naturally hesitant or even fearful in uncertain situations. This session will give us perspective on what Heaven is like.

We have included *Reflections* at the end of each session that correlate to Randy Alcorn's *50 Days of Heaven* book. We have provided space at the end of each *Reflection* where you can write your thoughts. These pages are for personal reflection that will not be shared during group time.

Open your group with prayer.

CONNECTING WITH GOD'S FAMILY (10 MIN.)

1 Read through the Group Values panel on the next page. Take some time to reflect on these values together. Choose one or two values to emphasize during this study—values that will take your group to the next stage of intimacy and spiritual health.

2 What do you think Heaven is like?
_____
_____
_____

3 How do you think Heaven compares to our lives here on earth?
_____
_____
_____

4 Who do you think will be in Heaven?
_____
_____
_____
_____

Roll Tape: DVD Session Nine

Watch the DVD teaching for this session now. After watching the video, have someone read the discussion questions in the *Growing* section and direct the group discussion.

GROWING TO BE LIKE CHRIST (30 MIN.)

Randy Alcorn's books, *Heaven* and *50 Days of Heaven*, were born out of his realization that many people don't really know what Heaven is like. Randy desires to give us purpose, perspective, and hope as we look forward to eternity in a real, tangible Heaven.

If you have a copy of *Heaven*, you may want to refer to the references included below as you answer the questions.

> **Group Values**
>
> **Attendance.** Give priority to the group meeting. Call or email if you will be late or absent.
>
> **Environment.** Help create a safe place where people can be heard and feel loved. (No quick answers, snap judgments, or simple fixes.)
>
> **Respect.** Be gentle and gracious—people have different spiritual maturity, personal opinions, and temperaments. Remember, we are all works in progress.
>
> **Confidentiality.** Keep everything that is shared in the group strictly confidential—no exceptions.
>
> **Welcome Newcomers.** Keep an open chair and share Jesus' dream of finding a shepherd for every sheep.
>
> **Group Ownership.** Remember that every member is a minister. Each group member should take on a small role or responsibility in the group over time.

5 Based on the video teaching, how has your perspective of Heaven changed?
_____
_____
_____
_____

Identify and discuss some of the misconceptions people have about Heaven. (*Heaven*, pp. 5–13)
_____
_____
_____
_____

6 In Isaiah 65:17a God says *Behold, I will create new heavens and a new earth* (NIV).

How does this verse help you see Heaven as a real place? What do you think the New Earth will look like? What will we look like? (*Heaven*, pp. 51–63)

_____

_____

_____

_____

7 One of the criminals crucified with Jesus said to him, *"Jesus, remember me when you come into your kingdom."* Jesus answered him, *"I tell you the truth, today you will be with me in Paradise."* Luke 23:42b-43 (NIV)

Where is Jesus now according to this verse? What does this say about where believers currently go when they die?

_____

_____

_____

_____

8 One of the biggest misconceptions is that the current Heaven, or Paradise, is our final destination when we die.

Read Revelation 21:2-3 and discuss where God will ultimately dwell with humankind. (*Heaven*, pp. 41–42)

_____

_____

_____

_____

We tend to picture the permanent Heaven rather than the temporary one. How does the dwelling place described in Revelation 21:2–3 differ from most people's understanding of Heaven?

_____

_____

_____

9 A New Jerusalem, on the New Earth, will be the dwelling place of all God's children after the Resurrection (see the timeline in the *Introduction*.) Take turns reading Isaiah 65:17–25.

According to this passage, what kind of place will the New Earth be? How important is this to you? Why? (*Heaven*, pp. 95–99)

_____
_____
_____
_____

10 *For since the creation of the world God's invisible qualities—his eternal power and divine nature—have been clearly seen, being understood from what has been made, so that men are without excuse.* Romans 1:20 (NIV)

Romans 1:20 speaks of how we can see God today. According to this scripture, how is God revealed to us? How does God reveal Himself to you?

_____
_____
_____
_____

11 Speaking of the New Jerusalem, John said in Revelation 21:26–27, *And all the nations will bring their glory and honor into the city. Nothing evil will be allowed to enter, nor anyone who practices shameful idolatry and dishonesty—but only those whose names are written in the Lamb's Book of Life* (NLT).

Enter through the narrow gate. For wide is the gate and broad is the road that leads to destruction, and many enter through it. But small is the gate and narrow the road that leads to life, and only a few find it. Matthew 7:13–14 (NIV)

After hearing Randy's teaching today, and reading the verses above, what is the default destination for unbelievers when they die? (*Heaven*, pp. 23–29)

_____
_____
_____
_____

12 Job said *I know that my Redeemer lives, and that in the end he will stand upon the earth. And after my skin has been destroyed, yet in my flesh I will see God . . .* Job 19:25–26 (NIV)

How does this verse give you assurance that you can live for eternity with the Lord?

_____
_____
_____

SHARING YOUR LIFE MISSION EVERY DAY (15 MIN.)

We can live with optimism and hope in the midst of all the sin in the world because of Jesus' redemptive work on the cross.

13 Jesus took our sin upon Himself, paying the price on our behalf, so that we can be with Him for all eternity.

Since the default destination of unbelievers is hell, what should be our mission?

_____
_____
_____
_____

14 The Bible says, *Since, then, you have been raised with Christ, set your hearts on things above, where Christ is seated at the right hand of God. Set your minds on things above, not on earthly things. For you died, and your life is now hidden with Christ in God.* Colossians 3:1–3 (NIV)

God says *Set your minds on things above . . .* How do you think living your life with an eternal perspective would affect the way you live your life each day?

_____
_____
_____
_____

15 Take a look at the *Circles of Life* diagram on page 115 of the Appendix and write in each circle the names of two or three people you know who need to connect in a Christian community like your small group. Commit to praying for God's guidance and an opportunity to invite them to your next group meeting.

PRAYER AND SURRENDER (10 MIN.)

16 This study has revealed many ideas about what Heaven is and is not. You may be surprised about or even disagree with what you've heard. Take a few minutes to pray for your response to this study. Also, ask God to help you find answers to any questions you still have regarding what Heaven is really like.

17 Share prayer requests in your group and the requests and praises on the *Prayer and Praise Report* beginning on page 116 in the Appendix. Commit to praying for each other throughout the week between group meetings.

Note: The contents of the *Reflections* at the end of the session correlate to Randy Alcorn's *50 Days of Heaven* book. We have provided space at the end of each *Reflection* where you can write your thoughts. These pages are for personal reflection that will not be shared during group time.

SCRIPTURE STUDY

If you want to dig deeper into the Bible passages about the topic at hand, we've provided suggested study passages below. The *Growing* section provides you with plenty to discuss within the group, so we recommend that participants study these passages on their own between group meetings, if desired.

- Colossians 3:1–3
- 1 Corinthians 15:55
- 2 Corinthians 5:6–8
- Ephesians 1:10; 2:8–9
- Exodus 33:18–23
- Galatians 3:13–14
- Genesis 3:8
- Habakkuk 1:13
- Hebrews 2:14–15; 11:16; 12:14; 13:8
- Isaiah 59:2; 65:17–25
- Job 19:25–27

- 1 John 1:9
- John 1:14; 10:30; 14:2, 9, 23; 16:33
- Luke 2:36–38; 10:20; 15:8; 16:19–31; 19:10
- Matthew 1:23, 5:8; 7:12–14; 8:12; 13:45; 17:12; 25:46
- 1 Peter 1:18–19; 3:18
- 2 Peter 3:13
- Philippians 1:21–23; 3:12–14
- Proverbs 28:13
- Psalm 19:1; 27:4; 42:1–2; 63:1; 73:25
- Revelation 21–22
- Romans 1:20; 3:23; 8:20–25, 32
- Romans 12:2
- 1 Timothy 6:16–17
- Titus 3:5

REFLECTIONS

Day 1 — If We Can Just See the Shore

If we can learn to fix our eyes on Jesus, to see through the fog of our present trials and circumstances, and picture our eternal home in our mind's eye, it will comfort and energize us, giving us a clear view of the shore—our eternal destination. Like the apostle Paul, we are encouraged to forget what is behind and press on toward the goal to win the prize.

Use the space included for each day to write down any thoughts or feelings that God is putting on your heart.

No, dear brothers and sisters, I am still not all I should be, but I am focusing all my energies on this one thing: Forgetting the past and looking forward to what lies ahead, I strain to reach the end of the race and receive the prize for which God, through Christ Jesus, is calling us up to heaven. Philippians 3:13–14 (NLT)

Reflection: Are you able to see the shore? What is God revealing to you?

_____
_____
_____
_____
_____
_____
_____
_____
_____
_____

MORE INFORMATION ABOUT THIS STUDY

This sample is the first session from the seven-session series *Heaven: Group Discussion Guide* by Randy Alcorn. The book is published by Tyndale House Publishers and the study series was developed by LifeTogether Publishing and Lamplighter Media. Both the book and the study series are available online through Christian Book Distributors or at your local Christian bookstore.

Author

Randy Alcorn is an author and the founder of Eternal Perspective Ministries (EPM), a nonprofit ministry dedicated to teaching principles of God's Word and assisting the church in ministering to unreached, unfed, unborn, uneducated, unreconciled, and unsupported people around the world. His ministry focus is communicating the strategic importance of using our earthly time, money, possessions, and opportunities to invest in ministries that count for eternity. He accomplishes this by analyzing, teaching, and applying the biblical truth. Before founding EPM in 1990, Randy served as a pastor for fourteen years. He holds degrees in theology and biblical studies and has taught on the adjunct faculties of Multnomah University and Western Seminary in Portland, Oregon. Randy has written more than forty books, including the bestsellers *Heaven*, *The Treasure Principle*, and the Gold Medallion winner *Safely Home*. His books in print exceed five million and have been translated into over thirty languages.

SESSION TEN
One Month to Live

Living the Dash
by Kerry and Chris Shook

If you had only one month left in your life, what would you do? Whether it's actually one month or an entire lifetime, every person has a limited amount of time to make a mark on history. When you look at tombstones, you see the date people were born and the date when they died. The significant contribution of these lives, however, is marked by the dash between those two dates.

How do you live a life without regrets? How do you take hold of the things God has called you to do? You have a choice in how the dash is going to be lived. A life surrendered to God will have a much greater impact than a life lived for self. But, where's the balance? This session will point you toward the wisdom to live a life pleasing to God.

1 What is the biggest risk you have ever taken?
_____
_____
_____

2 How did it make you feel? What was the outcome?
_____
_____
_____

3 When you were younger, what did you dream of becoming when you grew up?
_____
_____
_____

4 Looking back on your life, what is the best decision you have ever made? Why?

_____
_____
_____

LAUNCH POINT

Death is the great equalizer. It reaches the rich and the poor, the young and the old. No matter who you are you cannot escape death. This reality terrifies many people. For them, the fear of dying often prevents them from truly living. It cripples their dreams and prohibits them from taking risks in this life. For many, each passing day represents another missed opportunity, and moves them one step closer to the completion of a life that they fear may have been lived so incompletely. Yet if we were to stop for a moment and consider the fact that this life will be over one day, we may discover great truths about what it really means to live today.

The sum of one's life comes down to a few simple markings on their gravestone. Some have Bible verses and other facts or memorable sayings. All gravestones, however, have etched deep into them two dates separated by a dash. The dates represent the beginning and the end, while the dash represents a lifetime. It all comes down to the dash. There's not a lot we have control over in life—when were are born, and to whom we are born. But we do have control over what that dash will represent. We do get to decide how we're going to use our dash.

What if we knew our days were numbered?

Roll Tape: DVD Session Ten

GROUP DISCUSSION

1 How are we set free to be fully alive by considering that our time on earth is short?

_____
_____
_____

2 The clarifying question throughout this study is "What would I do if I knew I had one month to live?" How does this help clarify priorities and give us a new perspective on our time here on earth?

_____
_____
_____

3 Kerry said, *"There's so much life that is completely out of our control, but there is one thing that we do get to control. There is one thing that we do get to choose. We get to choose how to spend the dash between the two dates on our tombstones."* Discuss this idea as a group.

_____
_____
_____

4 What impressed you about how the man whose cancer had returned handled the news that he only had six to ten weeks to live? How did it change his relationship with his wife?

_____
_____
_____

We are given one life to live, one dash to define. Our time on earth is limited and our days are numbered. So how do we capitalize on the time we have been given? How are we to handle the gift of life God has blessed us with? As a group, consider what the following verses reveal about embracing our time on this earth as a limited resource.

1 Read Psalm 90:12 (Group or Individual Study)

What does it mean to *"number our days"*? What is the connection between numbering our days and gaining *"a heart of wisdom"*?

_____
_____
_____
_____

85

Exploring Deeper: Read James 3:13–18

How does verse 13 say wisdom is evidenced in a person's life?

_____
_____
_____
_____

The phrases *"bitter envy"* and *"selfish ambition"* are used in verses 14 and 16 to describe the root of *"earthly"* wisdom. Why do you think these terms are used?

How do verses 17–18 describe the wisdom that "comes from heaven"?

_____
_____
_____
_____

THINK ABOUT IT

If you knew you had one month to live, how might you live more wisely?

_____
_____
_____
_____

2 Read Psalm 39:4–5 (Group or Individual Study)

The Psalmist declares to God, "... the span of my years is as nothing before you." (NIV)

In light of the brevity of our lives here on earth, how should we embrace each day we are given?

_____
_____
_____
_____

If the whole of our lives is but *"a breath"* in the sight of God, what does this say about God, man, and eternity?

_____
_____
_____

Exploring Deeper: Read Philippians 3:20 and 1 Peter 2:11

Discuss what these passages say about the true home of all believers. Why are words like *"citizenship,"* *"aliens,"* and *"strangers"* used?

_____
_____
_____
_____

What implications does this have on how we spend our lives here on this earth? In light of our heavenly citizenship, how are we to conduct ourselves as residents on this earth?

_____
_____
_____
_____

THINK ABOUT IT

If you knew you had one month to live, how would that change your perspective on the time you have here on earth in relation to all of eternity?

_____
_____
_____
_____

3 Read 1 Peter 1:24–25 (Group or Individual Study)

What do we learn about the *"glory"* (beauty, strength, success) of man from this passage? Why do you think the imagery of grass and flowers is used?

_____
_____
_____
_____

How does the frailty of human life compare to the enduring nature of the word of God?

_____
_____
_____
_____

Exploring Deeper: Read Psalm 119:105, 2 Timothy 3:16–17, and Hebrews 4:12

Which passage uses the metaphor of a sword to describe the word of God? Why is this imagery used?

_____
_____
_____
_____

Which passage describes the word of God as a guiding light?

_____
_____

Which passage refers to the word of God as a teaching and training tool? What does this verse say is the intended result of being corrected and rebuked by the word of God?

_____
_____
_____

THINK ABOUT IT

If you knew you had one month to live, how would that change the way you approached and applied the word of God?

_____

_____

_____

PERSONAL APPLICATION

1 Without thinking too much, very quickly write down five things you would change about your life if you knew you only had one month to live.

1. _____
2. _____
3. _____
4. _____
5. _____

2 Identify one area of your life (e.g., the way you spend your time, the way you spend your money, a relationship that needs to be reconciled, etc.) and set a realistic goal for yourself in this particular area. Before your next group meeting, share your goal with your spouse or a close friend and ask them to help you and to hold you accountable in achieving your goal.

3 Commit to engaging in the *One Month to Live* Lifestyle for the next thirty days. Record your thoughts on how this lifestyle is affecting your relationships, your work, your family and your relationship with God in a planner or journal. Share your findings with your spouse or a close friend at the end of the thirty days.

What do you want the "dash" on your gravestone to represent? Prayerfully consider writing a one-sentence mission statement for your life. Post your mission statement in various places (e.g., your car, your desk, your bathroom mirror, etc.) so that you are reminded of it on a daily basis.

> *"Wouldn't it be wonderful to live your life so that if you discovered you only had a month to live, you wouldn't have to change a thing?"*
>
> —from *One Month to Live*

MORE INFORMATION ABOUT THIS STUDY

This sample is the first session from the six-session series *One Month to Live* by Kerry Shook. The book, study guides, and series are published by WaterBrook Press and are available online through Christian Book Distributors or at your local Christian bookstore.

Authors

Kerry and his wife Chris Shook are among today's most gifted communicators. They offer a clear, contemporary and creative teaching style. Kerry is the senior pastor of Woodlands Church, one of the fastest-growing churches in America. Kerry and Chris founded Fellowship of The Woodlands, now Woodlands Church, in 1993. Since then, the church has grown to 17,000 in average attendance each weekend. Woodlands Church is one church in many locations besides its Fellowship campus in The Woodlands outside of Houston, Texas; it also has satellite campuses in the Humble/Kingwood/Atascocita area, the Tomball area, and a new location in the Katy area. Future satellites are in the planning stages.

SESSION ELEVEN
Living on the Edge

God's Dream for Your Life
by Chip Ingram

Every person's life is surrounded by relationships. Each relationship influences you, and you in turn influence them. Some relationships bring out the best in you. Others definitely bring out the worst. Yet there is significance in each relationship that reflects what's going on inside of you.

There's a big difference between hearing great teaching and living great teaching. In this session on the book of Romans, Chip Ingram unpacks the nature of true spirituality. The apostle Paul moves from instruction to the practical application of his teaching. Each person has five relationships that will be dramatically impacted if you truly follow Jesus Christ.

Just like we have dreams for our kids, God has a dream for His children. More than God's dream being about what we do or the kind of job we have, His dream is about the kind of person we will become. But what kind of person does He want us to become? We could spend a lot of time offering our opinions and ideas or we could let God speak for Himself. In this opening session, Chip gives us an overview of an authentic Christ-follower that comes straight from Scripture. Let the journey begin.

Roll Tape: DVD Session Eleven

Every parent has a dream for their _____.

Our kids can be a source of great _____ or immeasurable _____.

Your heavenly Father has a _____ for you.

The LORD your God is with you, he is mighty to save. He will take great delight in you, he will quiet you with his love, he will rejoice over you with singing. (Zephaniah 3:17 NIV)

God's big agenda

Developing your _____ and making you like His Son.

MORE IMPORTANT THAN WHAT YOU DO IS WHAT YOU BECOME.

A Christ-follower (disciple) is not defined by

_____
_____
_____

Romans 12—The executive summary of an authentic Christ-follower.

GOD'S DREAM IS THAT CHRISTIANS WOULD ACTUALLY LIVE LIKE CHRISTIANS.

Your relationship with _____ . . . Surrendered to God (v. 1)

_____

Your relationship with the _____ . . . Separate from the world (v. 2)

_____

Your relationship with _____ . . . Sober in self-assessment (vv. 3–8)

_____

Your relationship with _____ . . . Serving in love (vv. 9–13)

_____

Your relationship to _____ . . . Supernaturally responding to evil with good (vv. 14–21)

TALK IT OVER

1 When you were growing up, what did it mean to be a good Christian?

2 Chip talked about God being a heavenly Father who has a dream for us. As you were growing up, what was your view of God?

What was He like?

How has your understanding of God changed?

3 In your opinion, why are so many Christians stuck and not growing spiritually?

4 How is spiritual maturity defined in your church?

If you were trying to describe the road to spiritual maturity to a brand new Christian, how would you describe it?

_____
_____
_____

5 Over the course of your Christian life, who or what has had the most impact on your spiritual growth?

_____
_____
_____

6 How would you describe your spiritual growth over the last five years?

_____
_____
_____

When did you grow the most?

_____
_____
_____

7 How satisfied are you with your spiritual growth?

⟵————————————————————⟶
1 2 3 4 5 6 7 8 9 10

Unhealthy   Healthy

LIVE IT OUT

Read Romans 12 every day this week. This can be done in less than five minutes each day.

MORE INFORMATION ABOUT THIS STUDY

This sample is the first session from the ten-session series *Living on the Edge* by Chip Ingram. The study guides and series are published by Living on the Edge and available online through Christian Book Distributors or at your local Christian bookstore.

Author

Chip Ingram's passion is to help Christians really live like Christians. As a pastor, author, coach and teacher for more than twenty-five years, Chip has helped people around the world break out of spiritual ruts and live out God's purpose for their lives. Today Chip serves as senior pastor of Venture Christian Church in Los Gatos, California, and president of Living on the Edge, an international teaching and discipleship ministry. Over the last twenty-five years Chip has pastored churches ranging from 500 to 5,000 and served as president of Walk through the Bible. Chip holds an M.S. degree from West Virginia University and a Th.M. degree from Dallas Theological Seminary. He is the author of eleven books, including his newest releases *Living on the Edge*, *Overcoming Emotions That Destroy*, and *Holy Ambition*. Reaching more than a million people a week, his teaching can be heard online and through hundreds of radio and television outlets worldwide. Chip and his wife, Theresa, have four children and eight grandchildren.

SESSION TWELVE
90 Minutes in Heaven

Heaven in the Next Instant?
by Don Piper

Pastor Don Piper got a few brief moments at the gates of heaven after he was in a deadly car accident where his car was run over by a semi truck. Crushed and trapped in his vehicle, he was pronounced dead at the scene.

An hour and a half later, something happened, and Don returned mysteriously to life. This lesson reflects on his account of the events that occurred during that tragic and amazing day. Prepare to have your ideas about heaven and your views of God made clearer as you spend today's session with Don Piper.

"You have decided the length of our lives. You know how many months we will live, and we are not given a minute longer." —Job 14:5 (NLT)

Roll Tape: DVD Session Twelve

HOW I DIED AND LIVED TO TELL ABOUT IT

Shortly after I left a ministerial conference in East Texas to return home to Houston, an eighteen-wheeler veered into my lane and hit my car head-on. The EMTs pronounced me dead on the scene. Instantly upon impact, I found myself in heaven, a place of indescribable beauty, love, reunion, glorious music, perfection, and ecstasy. I'll tell you more about that later.

Minutes later, another pastor who had been at the conference, Dick Onerecker, arrived at the scene; he stopped, wanting to pray for the injured. The medics told him I was dead, but Dick still felt a strong urging from God, so he crawled into what remained of the car, put his hand on my shoulder, and prayed. After a while he began to sing a hymn, and to his great surprise, I began to sing with him.

Dick convinced the incredulous EMTs to come to the car. They found a pulse and rushed me from hospital to hospital to keep me alive until they finally reached

Hermann Hospital in Houston, six and a half hours after the accident. Word went out to churches everywhere, and thousands of Christians began interceding for my life.

My injuries were extensive and critical, to say the least. Large hunks of bone were missing from my leg and arm, and doctors feared those limbs were beyond saving. But a new device designed to stimulate bone regrowth—the Ilizarov frame—had recently been approved for use in the U.S. The process promised to be long and painful, but I was unconscious, and my wife made the decision to apply the device.

I endured a grueling two-year recovery, including thirteen months in the hospital and thirty-four operations. Often I prayed that God would take me back to heaven. When that didn't happen, I grew despondent because I could find no meaning in seemingly endless months of suffering.

But eventually I did find meaning, thanks to the help of a friend. Even more, I found new purpose for my life and a ministry that has become my mission and passion. Thousands have been helped by my testimony about heaven, and have turned to God's Word because of it—which is where this study will be focused.

COMING TO TERMS WITH REALITY

Almost all of us have some sort of outline for the story of our life, with certain elements in common: a satisfying career, a good education, a happy marriage, obedient children, a nice home, money in the bank, adorable grandchildren, and a comfortable retirement.

I was no exception. I was thirty-eight years old and in good health with my future set. My story was moving along according to plan. When I left that conference in East Texas, I had no idea that my world was about to be smashed into chaos.

While my experience after that collision was unique in one way—few people who die and go to heaven come back to tell about it—in other ways, it is common to just about everyone. Life isn't obligated to follow our outline. We make decisions, large and small, which we think will lead to one result but which often lead instead to something utterly unexpected. When I decided to take a new route home that day, little did I know how far-reaching the results would be.

We sometimes make other, less innocent decisions that lead to grave consequences, such as Adam and Eve's choice in the Garden of Eden. God's gift of freedom to make decisions is a tremendous one. But at the same time, He has placed us in a position of high responsibility where everything we do has wide ramifications in our work, our relationships, our worship. We exercise our God-given responsibility in these areas by making decisions, and God gives us great leeway in making them—even to the point of allowing us to occasionally make disastrous choices.

Even if we do habitually seek God's wisdom so as to avoid most self-imposed consequences, occasionally we are victims of plot spoilers beyond our control—some caused by the choices of others and some by acts of nature. Accidents, diseases, divorces, job losses, family deaths, financial ruin—eventually everyone runs up against such unexpected twists. Obviously, Christians are not exempt from the effects of evil. We face the same uncertainties about the next minute as unbelievers.

I used to think it was a cliché to say that life is uncertain, but now I think we don't say it enough. No matter how detailed our plans, how lofty our dreams, or how elaborate the structures of our lives, at any moment those plans can be scrambled, those dreams can collapse, and construction on our life project can grind to a halt. Too many people, however, are living as if they don't believe it. But it's true; I can literally feel it in my bones!

The biggest plot spoiler of them all, of course, is death. It awaits everyone, lurking around some unknown corner, ready to ambush you and end your story, often long before you would prefer to conclude the chapters. And that is why we fear it: since Enoch and Elijah, the death rate among humans has been 100 percent. A quarter million people leave this planet every day, with every one of us a guaranteed future customer at the local mortuary.

In the face of our fear, it would be easy to just throw up our hands and say, "What's the use in trying if life is so uncertain that no endeavor is assured of completion?" But we who trust God and submit to Him will work to fulfill our calling and accomplish His will on earth, not because we expect to finish all we set out to do, but because God wants to see us in action as if the earth were not under the curse of the Fall. As the parable of the talents (Matthew 25:14–30) illustrates, when we plan and work in spite of life's uncertainty, we are demonstrating our willingness to be what we were created to be—God's agents, bearing His Spirit, accepting His grace, and diligently going about His business. In return, God gives us assurance of heaven. His promise of a certain eternity is the antidote to despair, providing hope, meaning, and joy to an uncertain today.

So instead of viewing our lives as a futile quest, or pushing thoughts of our mortality aside as too dreadful to think about, we should prepare for what's to come just as one prepares for surgery to cure a life-threatening disease. You and I suffer from the fatal tumor of sin, and the Master Surgeon stands ready to cut it away and restore us to perfection. Doesn't it make sense to prepare for *that* operation in the same way we would prepare for one at our local hospital? Shouldn't we follow the Surgeon's directives so that when the time comes, we'll be ready?

Death certainly isn't good. It was inflicted on us by our archenemy Satan. God hates it. Christ wept over it. Paul calls it an enemy. Yet because of Christ's sacrifice and resurrection, the curse of death has been transformed. Death still strikes, but its poison is no longer deadly. Thanks to Christ, it not only frees us from the suffering and uncertainties of this life, but it is now our passageway to new life in heaven, where we will spend eternity in the presence of God. This is why the apostle Paul anticipated death and even yearned for it (2 Corinthians 5:8–9). If we focus on the cure—the new life—it will help us overcome our fear of the surgical process itself.

I find it significant that all cultures in history have believed in some sort of afterlife. God has planted the idea in the human consciousness and given every person an innate desire to be with Him after death. Without Jesus and salvation, heaven becomes a mere wish for the future, but for believers it is a surety.

The Bible affirms the validity of this belief and gives us tantalizing hints of the nature of paradise. And I can personally attest to the reality of heaven's splendor. In fact, my vivid experience in heaven is one of the things that snapped me out of my apprehension. I *know* heaven is real because I've tasted its wonders. Now I am eager to return, and that longing—along with wanting to escape the pain and suffering I've endured throughout my long recovery—has obliterated all fear of death.

Being convinced of heaven is not only the most effective way to cope with the plot spoilers we must endure in our personal stories, but it gives us enormous power to live in this present world. My assurance of heaven has given me a new ministry and a new purpose. In fact, I'm convinced that this is why God sent me back. When I left my hospital bed thirteen months after the accident, excruciating pain and memories of heaven are the two things I carried with me that motivated me to communicate hope to suffering people. This ability to bless others is how my anticipation of heaven gives me power to live now.

Conviction of heaven can also give us power over a long list of things that often tempt us to spoil our own stories—fads and fashions, conformity with cultural values, peer pressure, lust and materialism. These temptations won't affect a person with a strong assurance of heaven any more than a quick hot dog would tempt a person who knows a steak dinner with all the trimmings awaits at home.

Some people wonder, though, if achieving a good life now is more important than anticipating heaven. Isn't it wrong to emphasize a future in heaven, they ask, when we have a society to improve and a planet to save here and now? Doesn't heavenly-mindedness selfishly put the focus on personal reward rather than the good of humankind?

Yes, it's mercenary to seek a self-serving reward, but not a reward appropriate to our legitimate endeavors. The proper reward for hard work is a nice paycheck. The proper reward for diligent studies is a good grade. The proper reward for a Christian is to hear "welcome home" from the smiling lips of our Father.

And it's true that we are charged to do our best to improve our world; Jesus urged us to become its preserving salt and guiding light. It's also true that some Christians seem to be so eternally-minded that they are of no earthly good. But Christians are right to emphasize heaven. Anticipation of it saturates the pages of the New Testament and the writings of the early Christian fathers. They spoke of it, wrote of it, longed for it. And that anticipation gave them power to live their present lives joyfully, without fear of the unexpected.

Heaven made them bold and courageous. Death might be imminent, but it was not permanent, and they knew a better world awaited—a world free of all suffering, free of all fear, free of death. A world where no story ever ends.

That is what my experiences have taught me as well. I have been shown that heaven is real, but the reality of heaven doesn't matter if you're not going. So, in this study, I invite you to come along. I want to help you get there, and I want to help you *want* to get there. I want to show you that you can have a better life here if heaven becomes a firm reality to you.

1 People change, and so do their stories. As a child, what did you want to be when you grew up? What are some of the unexpected turns your life has taken?

_____
_____
_____
_____

2 Have you ever been in a situation where you thought you were about to die? How did that experience affect you at the time? What about now?

_____
_____
_____
_____

3 Read James 5:16. Obviously, God could have revived Don without Dick Onerecker's prayer. So why did God have Dick pray for Don?

_____
_____
_____

4 Though He loves us and cares about our well-being, God gives us no assurance of mortal life past the present moment. Why do you think that is?

_____
_____
_____

5 Look up James 4:14. How does the temporary, uncertain nature of life affect your attitude toward the present and your thinking about the future?

_____
_____
_____

6 Reflect on what Jesus said in Matthew 6:33–34 and respond.

_____
_____
_____

The top priorities in my life, in descending order, are:

_____
_____
_____
_____

Of these priorities, the one to which I would sacrifice all others is:

_____

_____

_____

LIVE WHAT YOU'VE LEARNED

In seventeenth-century England, it was customary for the church to toll a funeral bell for the death of a Christian. John Donne famously wrote, "Ask not for whom the bell toll; it tolls for thee." Today, as an exercise in acclimatizing yourself to the certainty of death, every time you hear a bell or buzzer—be that a phone, church chimes, a computer notification, and elevator stopping, or a doorbell—think of it as Donne's bell tolling for you. Then stop for a moment and utter a prayer of thanks to God that He has transformed death from a grave into a passage.

MORE INFORMATION ABOUT THIS STUDY

This sample is the first session from the seven-session series *90 Minutes in Heaven* by Don Piper. The book is published by Revell; the study guides and series are published by Worthy Resources. The book and series are available online through Christian Book Distributors or at your local Christian bookstore.

Author

Don Piper has mesmerized and inspired nearly three thousand audiences around the globe since the release of his best-selling book in 2004. Millions have experienced the *90 Minutes in Heaven* story in person, on television, radio, and print media. Don Piper has sold over 5 million copies of his books in forty languages. His first book, *90 Minutes in Heaven: A True Story of Death and Life*, remained on the *New York Times* best-seller list for nearly four years! This book, from Revell, is widely considered to be a landmark book that has led to renewed interest in heaven.

BONUS SESSION
Building Biblical Community

Becoming a Celebrating Community
by Steve Gladen and Bill Donahue

What is a small group? How does a group get started? This lesson on Becoming a Celebrating Community *is a foundation piece in creating a small group. Steve Gladen from Saddleback Church and Bill Donahue from Willow Creek Community Church have launched thousands of groups with tens of thousands of group members, yet their hearts beat for each individual group and leader within a local church.*

This bonus session will give you tools for starting and sustaining your small group. Steve and Bill offer proven methods to develop true biblical community in your group. You will learn how to share life together and grow in your faith.

JOY IS CONTAGIOUS

Joy brightens the face and lifts the heart. The practice of celebration is indeed an expression of joy, something we do together that allows us to laugh at ourselves, accept our trials, and remember that God is still good.

It has been said that community is the place where the person you least like to be with always lives. We don't like to think about it, but there is some truth in that. We are called to love and connect with people we may not like, or who dislike us. It definitely takes maturity to love and build in that setting.

But there is another side to community—the part that invites us into generous, caring, joy-filled relationships. That is the fun, exciting aspect of meeting new friends, getting to learn new truths about God, the world, and ourselves, and coming together to play, laugh, and enjoy life.

Our desire is that your group becomes such a community. But that requires getting to know each other—your stories, dreams, personalities, passions, bumps, and bruises—so you can celebrate what God is doing in and through each other and the group itself.

Our goal for the first session is that you begin to learn more about one another so you can become a community that celebrates being together.

LEADER: (15 min.) Play Segment 1.1 and have group members share in the following experience.

Reflect on the statement below, jot down some notes, then discuss with the rest of the group.

1 I am attending this group because I hope/expect that . . .

_____
_____
_____
_____

You probably remember the first time you joined a group or a team. Perhaps it was a study group, a sports team, or your first work group. Or maybe it was just a group of kids you hung out with in the neighborhood.

2 What do you remember about that group or team? What made it fun to be a part of? If it wasn't fun, what was missing that would have made it so?

_____
_____
_____
_____

LEADER: (15 min.) Play Segment 1.2. In this segment, Bill and Steve describe why celebration is essential in building a life-changing community. Then have group members share in the following experience.

Place a mark on the continuum indicating your joy factor this week.

I am experiencing much joy. ————————————— Joy—what's that?

3 Explain why you find yourself there. What is it that stirs joy in you?

_____
_____
_____

LEADER: (15 min.) Play Segment 1.3 and then have group members share in the following experience.

Look at Acts 2:42–47 below and read it together. It mentions "a joyful and humble attitude" and a group of people who were "having favor with all the people" (NIV). Joy was at the center of this community.

> ⁴²And they devoted themselves to the apostles' teaching, to the fellowship, to the breaking of bread, and to the prayers.
>
> ⁴³Then fear came over everyone, and many wonders and signs were being performed through the apostles. ⁴⁴Now all the believers were together and held all things in common. ⁴⁵They sold their possessions and property and distributed the proceeds to all, as anyone had a need. ⁴⁶Every day they devoted themselves to meeting together in the temple complex, and broke bread from house to house. They ate their food with a joyful and humble attitude, ⁴⁷praising God and having favor with all the people. And every day the Lord added to them those who were being saved.

4 List some of the characteristics of this community that produced joy.

_____
_____
_____

5 What role do you think community activities played in fostering this atmosphere of joy? Where have you seen that in your own life?

_____
_____
_____

Joy may be a regular experience for you or perhaps at this moment the hassles of life just cloud it out. So think back for a moment and respond to the following question.

6 Describe a time when you felt built up, encouraged, and affirmed. For example, think back to a birthday celebration or maybe a graduation party. What did the people around you do that filled you with joy?

_____
_____
_____

LEADER: (15 min.) Play Segment 1.4. Then have group members share in the following experience.

Notes from Bill and Steve's Teaching

_____
_____
_____
_____
_____

THE PRACTICE OF CELEBRATION

Joy seems to revolve around three relationships: with God, self, and others. Usually we have cause to celebrate life in at least one of these relationships at any point in time. For now, let's reflect on "self." Focus on what's going on in your own life.

7 Take a moment to reflect on God's work in your life. What things can you celebrate? What could the group do to express joy for what God is doing or has done? Here are some ideas to get you started.

- Worship together by listening to some music and reflecting on God.
- Ask one or two people to tell stories of God's specific work in their lives.
- Give thanks: Ask everyone to finish the sentence, "I am so grateful to God because . . ."

LEADER: (15 min.) Play Segment 1.5 as a wrap-up to this session. Then have a group members answer the following question. Close with prayer.

8 What I learned or experienced during this meeting:

PRAYER REMINDERS

MORE INFORMATION ABOUT THIS STUDY

This sample is the first session from the four-session series *Building Biblical Community* by Steve Gladen and Bill Donahue. The study guides and series are published by Lifeway Publishers and available through LifeWay online and at your local Christian bookstore.

Authors

Steve Gladen joined the staff of Saddleback Church (www.saddleback.com) in February of 1998 as Pastor of Small Groups, where he oversees the strategic launch and development of the small group community. Steve also founded the Small Group Network, a network for leaders of small group ministry, in 2006 (www.smallgroupnetwork.com). Using the Great Commission and Great Commandment as inspiration, Steve encourages every group member to balance the five biblical purposes in their heart and groups. Steve does consulting and seminars throughout the United States and internationally, championing small groups and teaching what it means to have small groups with purpose. Learn more about Steve at www.smallgroups.net. Steve and his wife Lisa reside in Southern California, have been married since 1989, and have two children.

Bill Donahue is the Executive Director of small group ministries for the Willow Creek Association. He previously served on the staff of Willow Creek Community Church, helping to develop and launch the church-wide small group ministry. Coauthor with Russ Robinson of *Building a Church of Small Groups* and *The Seven Deadly Sins of Small Group Ministry*, he has edited or contributed to many Willow Creek small group Bible study guides, including the *Interactions* and *New Community* series. He currently leads a small group and lives in West Dundee, Illinois, with his wife, Gail, and their two children.

Appendix

SMALL GROUP FAQs

Who may attend this group?

Anybody you feel would benefit. As you begin, we encourage each attendee to invite at least one other friend to join. Take some time at your first meeting to share the names of people you hope to invite, and pray as a group that they might be open to attending. The best time to have people join the group is in the first or second week of a new study.

How long will this group meet?

Most studies are four, six, eight, or twelve weeks long, but we encourage groups to add one additional week for a final celebration. At the end of the study, each group member makes the decision whether to stay on for another study or leave the group. In your final session of a study, take time to discuss your Small Group Covenant (next page), and what study you plan to do next. This is a great time to discuss which of the *Best of Small Groups* studies you would like to sample study next.

Does this group need a leader? Who will the leader be?

Most groups have a leader. If you do not have a leader, take a few minutes to talk about who might fill this role in your group. We encourage you to select one or more discussion leaders, and recommend that you rotate the job of facilitator to create the opportunity for everyone to develop this skill. Several other responsibilities can be rotated, including refreshments, prayer requests, worship, and keeping up with those who miss a meeting. Shared ownership in the group helps everybody grow.

Where do we find new group members for our group?

This can be an issue for groups, especially new groups starting with just a few people, or existing groups that have lost a few members along the way. Brainstorm a list of people from your workplace, church, neighborhood, school, family, gym, and so on. Then pray for the people on each member's list. Have each group member invite several people on their list. No matter how you find members, it is important to continue actively looking for new people to join your group. All groups go through some healthy attrition as a result of people moving, ministry opportunities, and so forth. If the group gets too small, it runs the risk of shutting down. You never know—the next person you add might just become a friend for eternity.

How do we handle the childcare needs in our group?

This is a sensitive issue in groups. We suggest that you seek creative solutions as a group. One common solution is for the adults to meet in the living room while the kids gather in another part of the house. You can share the cost of a babysitter (or two) to be with the kids if necessary. Another popular option is to have one home for the kids and a second home (close by) for the adults. The adults might rotate the responsibility of providing a lesson for the kids. This last option is great with school-age kids, and can be a huge blessing to families.

What if we cannot get through all the content each week?

The curriculum is provided to serve you as a group and as a leader. Do not feel obligated to get through all the content in this study guide. Be sensitive to the leading of the Holy Spirit during your group meeting. Some items will be more applicable for your group than others. Choose those items that best fit your group life. However, if an item stretches you as a group, don't ignore it. New experiences will breathe new growth and community into your small group!

Many groups are able to complete each session in one meeting, while others take several extra weeks. Feel free to adjust your pace according to the needs of your group. If the need arises to take a week and give attention to needs in your group, do so—then come back to the study guide the following week. We encourage you to periodically meet together specifically for the purpose of building relationships within your group.

SMALL GROUP COVENANT

To be reviewed quarterly, or as needed.

Group Purpose

_____

_____

_____

As a group, we agree to the following disciplines:

Attendance   To give priority to the group meeting. *Call when absent or late.*

Safety   To help create a safe place where people can be heard. *No quick answers or judgments.*

Confidentiality   To keep anything that is shared strictly confidential. *What's said in this group, stays in this group.*

Accountability   To give permission to group members to hold you accountable to the goals you set for yourself.

Assimilation   To keep the door open to others—unconnected people in our church and unchurched people outside—who need what we have.

Rotation   To rotate hosting responsibilities for the meeting.

Responsibility   To take an active role in the responsibilities of this small group.

What we want to do about

Refreshments/Mealtimes

_____
_____

Childcare

_____
_____

When we will meet (day of the week and time)

_____
_____

Where we will meet (place)

_____
_____

We will begin at _____, and close at
_____.

We will study . . .

_____
_____

We will do our best (some or all of us) to attend the following service together:

_____
_____

SMALL GROUP CALENDAR

Healthy groups share responsibilities and group ownership. This usually happens progressively over time rather than overnight. Sharing responsibilities and ownership ensures that no one person carries the group alone. The calendar below can help you organize your group's shared responsibilities. You can also add a social event, mission project, birthdays, and days off to your calendar. This should be completed after your first or second meeting. Planning ahead will facilitate better attendance and greater involvement from others.

Date	Session	Host Home	Dessert/Meal	Leader

SMALL GROUP ROSTER

Name	Address	Phone	Email	Group Role	Church Ministry

CIRCLES OF LIFE

When starting a new group or renewing an existing group, it's helpful to have each member, starting with the group leader, prayerfully reflect on people they might invite to the group. Take a moment to write down as many names as you can in each one of the circles in your life. Then call several of them this week to see if they would like to join your group for your next study.

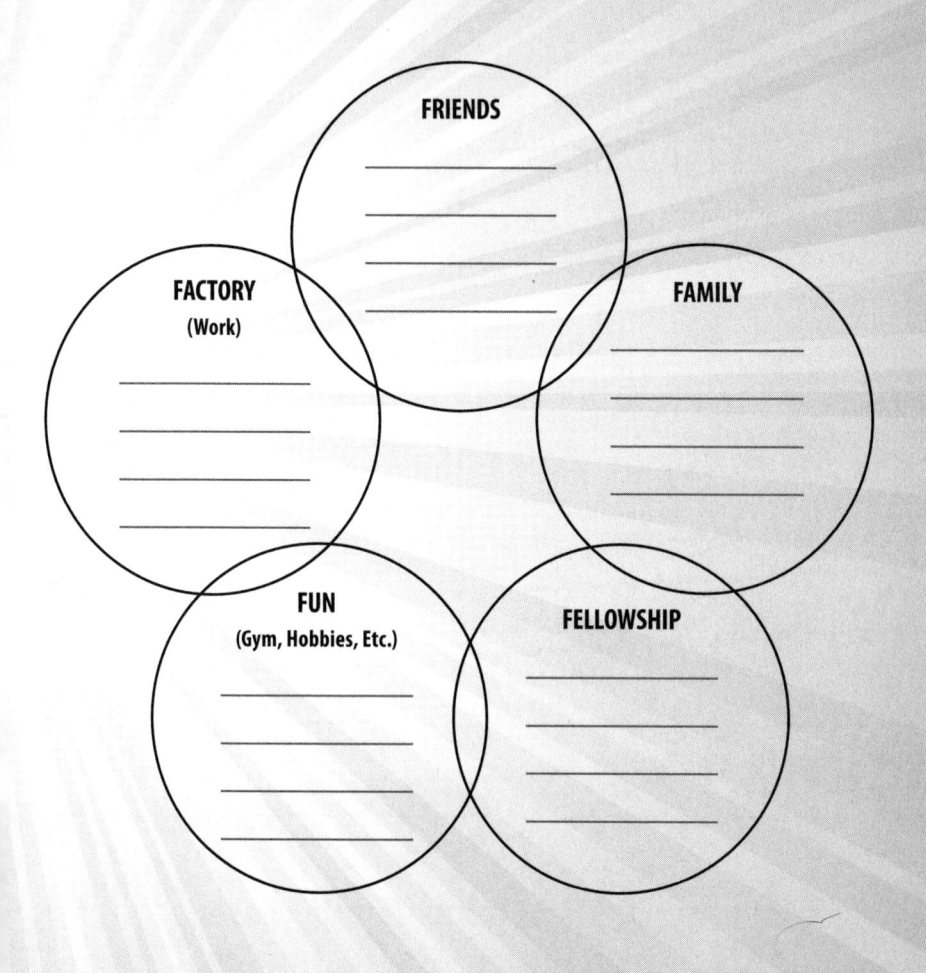

FRIENDS

FACTORY
(Work)

FAMILY

FUN
(Gym, Hobbies, Etc.)

FELLOWSHIP

PRAYER AND PRAISE REPORT

Briefly share your prayer requests with the large group, making notations below. Then gather in smaller groups of two to four to pray for each other.

Prayer Request	Praise Report

ABOUT BRETT EASTMAN AND LIFETOGETHER

Brett Eastman has produced, authored, or co-authored over 200 small group curriculum series including the bestselling Purpose Driven® Small Group curriculum, *Doing Life Together* (Zondervan), which has sold over 3,000,000 copies. He also was the primary designer behind the 40 Days of Purpose Campaigns that fueled over 25,000 churches around the world. Since then he has worked with many major Christian publishers to produce small group curricula for their top authors.

Brett Eastman started Lifetogether in 1999 after serving as the Small Group Champion at Saddleback Church and Willow Creek Community Church for over a decade. Lifetogether's mission is to catalyze a movement that transforms lives through community in order to help fulfill the Great Commandment and Great Commission in this generation. Lifetogether provides a variety of services, including curriculum production, campaign development and small group ministry coaching to churches of all sizes and denominations around the country. Lifetogether also distributes numerous free small group resources for small group and ministry leaders.

For more information about Brett Eastman and Lifetogether visit www.Lifetogether.com.

Additional Permissions

Scripture quotations marked (NIV) are taken from the HOLY BIBLE, NEW INTERNATIONAL VERSION®. Copyright 1973, 1978, and 1984 by International Bible Society. Used by permission of Zondervan Bible Publishing House. All rights reserved.

Scripture quotations marked (MESS) are taken from THE MESSAGE. © 1993, 1994, 1995, 1996, 2000, 2001, 2002 by Eugene H. Peterson. Used by permission of NavPress Publishing Group

Scripture quotations noted (NLT) are from THE HOLY BIBLE, NEW LIVING TRANSLATION®. Copyright 1996. Used by permission of Tyndale House Publishers, Inc., Wheaton, IL 60189. All rights reserved.

Scripture quotations noted (ESV) are taken from the HOLY BIBLE, ENGLISH STANDARD VERSION®. Copyright 2001 by Crossway Bibles, a publishing ministry of Good News Publishers. All rights reserved.

Scripture quotations noted (NCV) are taken from the New Century Version. Copyright © 1987, 1988, 1991 by Thomas Nelson, Inc. Used by permission.

Scripture quotations noted (NKJV) are taken from the New King James Version. Copyright © 1982 by Thomas Nelson, Inc. Used by permission. All rights reserved.

Respective sessions in *The Best of Small Groups* appear by permission of their individual publishers.

Session from *Making Room for Neighbors*
Copyright © 2010 by Oak Hills Church, San Antonio, Texas. Originally published in *Making Room for Neighbors* by Hendrickson Publishers, Peabody, Massachusetts 01961, U.S.A. Unauthorized Distribution Prohibited

Session from *Forgotten God*
Copyright © 2010 by Francis Chan and Mark Beuving. Originally published in *Forgotten God* by David C. Cook, Colorado Springs, Colorado 80918, U.S.A. Unauthorized Distribution Prohibited

Session from *Vintage Jesus*
Copyright © 2011 by Hudson Productions. Originally published in *Vintage Jesus* by The Hub, Dallas, Texas 75205, U.S.A. Unauthorized Distribution Prohibited

Session from *Not a Fan*
Copyright © 2010 by City on a Hill Studio, LLC. Originally Published in *Not a Fan* by City on a Hill Studio, Louisville, Kentucky 40223, U.S.A. Unauthorized Distribution Prohibited

Session from *Life's Toughest Questions*
Copyright © 2010 by Erwin McManus. Originally published in *Life's Toughest Questions* by LifeWay Christian Resources, Nashville, Tennessee 37234, U.S.A. Unauthorized Distribution Prohibited

Session from *When I Don't Desire God*
Copyright © 2008 by Desiring God. Originally published in *When I Don't Desire God* by Crossway Books, Wheaton, Illinois 60187, U.S.A. Unauthorized Distribution Prohibited

Session from *Guarding Your Child's Heart*
Copyright © 2011 by Gary Smalley. Originally published in *Guarding Your Child's Heart* by NavPress, Colorado Springs, Colorado 80935, U.S.A. Unauthorized Distribution Prohibited

Session from *DO Something!*
Copyright © 2009 by Miles McPherson. Originally published in *DO Something!* by Baker Books, a Division of Baker Book House Company, Grand Rapids, Michigan 49516, U.S.A. Unauthorized Distribution Prohibited

Session from *Heaven*
Copyright © 2008 by Lifetogether Publishing and Lamplighter Media. Originally published in *Heaven* by Lifetogether Publishers and Lamplighter Media, San Diego, CA 92126, U.S.A. Unauthorized Distribution Prohibited

Session from *One Month to Live*
Copyright © 2008 by One Month to Live Challenge. Originally published in *One Month to Live Challenge* by The One Month to Live Challenge, Ramona, California 92065, U.S.A. Unauthorized Distribution Prohibited

Session from *Living on the Edge*
Copyright © 2009 by Living on the Edge and Chip Ingram. Originally published in *Living on the Edge* by Living on the Edge, Suwanee, Georgia 30024 U.S.A. Unauthorized Distribution Prohibited.

Session from *90 Minutes in Heaven*
Copyright © 2004 by Don Piper. Originally published in *90 Minutes in Heaven* by Revell, a division of Baker Book House Company, Grand Rapids, Michigan 49516, U.S.A. Unauthorized Distribution Prohibited

Session from *Building Biblical Community*
Copyright © 2010 by Bill Donahue and Steve Gladen. Originally published in *Building Biblical Community* by LifeWay Christian Resources, Nashville, Tennessee 37234, U.S.A. Unauthorized Distribution Prohibited